SMART WOMEN
TAKE RISKS

SMART WOMEN TAKE RISKS

SIX STEPS FOR CONQUERING YOUR FEARS AND MAKING THE LEAP TO SUCCESS

HELENE LERNER

McGraw-Hill

New York   Chicago   San Francisco
Lisbon   London   Madrid   Mexico City
Milan   New Delhi   San Juan   Seoul
Singapore   Sydney   Toronto

The McGraw·Hill Companies

1 2 3 4 5 6 7 8 9 0   DOC/DOC   0 9 8 7 6

ISBN 0-07-146754-8

McGraw-Hill books are available at special quantity discounts to use as premiums and sales promotions, or for use in corporate training programs. For more information, please write to the Director of Special Sales, Professional Publishing, McGraw-Hill, Two Penn Plaza, New York, NY 10121-2298. Or contact your local bookstore.

Portions of this material are excerpted from *Our Power as Women: Wisdom and Strategies of Highly Successful Women*, by Helene Lerner, with permission of Conari Press, an imprint of Red Wheel/Weiser.

The quotes and testimonies in this book express the personal points of view of the women who shared them. They should not in any way be interpreted as or construed to be the views of the organizations or entities with which they are affiliated. Titles and affiliations are for identification purposes only. The views and opinions of the individuals interviewed for this book are not necessarily the same views held by the author. She has included them to give the reader the broadest possible scope as to how various people view the subject of the book.

The author in certain cases used as examples women who are not actual people, but represent a composite of her experiences with colleagues, clients, friends, and acquaintances.

For more insights on advancement, leadership, and risk-taking, go to www.womenworking.com.

*I dedicate this book to the many women
who shared their insights with me
through the years and all those readers
who will be benefiting
from their wisdom.*

CONTENTS

	Acknowledgments	*ix*
	It's Time for You to Take Smart Risks	*xi*
Preface	*Live in the Leap*	*xiii*
Part One	FOLLOW THE SIX-STEP PROGRAM	1
Step One	COMMIT TO YOUR GOAL	3
Step Two	CALCULATE—DETERMINE YOUR RISK QUOTIENT	31
Step Three	TEAM WITH WINNERS	59
Step Four	TAKE A LEAP AND COME FROM STRENGTH	79
Step Five	CLAIM VICTORY—YOU'VE EARNED IT	97
Step Six	DON'T STOP—SUCCESS BREEDS SUCCESS	107
Part Two	TRIUMPH WITH VICTORIOUS MENTORS: SUCCESSFUL WOMEN WHO TAKE SMART RISKS AND SHARE THEIR STORIES	119
	Dolores Morris, Vice President, HBO Family & Documentary Programming	123
	Louise Francesconi, Vice President, Raytheon Company; President, Raytheon Missile Systems	127

Sheila Schectman, CEO,   131
Giftcorp, Inc.

Lynn Laverty Elsenhans, Executive   133
Vice President, Global Manufacturing,
Shell Downstream Inc.

Margo Gray, President,   137
Horizon Engineering Services Company

Anna Catalano, Executive Coach   141
& Entrepreneur

Jan Babiak, Managing Partner   145
of Technology and Security Risk Services,
Ernst & Young LLP, U.K.

Lynn Davenport, Claim Team Manager,   149
State Farm

Stephanie Moore, Vice President,   151
Human Resources, BP,
Exploration & Production Technology

Sheila Cluff, Founder & Owner,   155
Fitness Inc., The Oaks at Ojai

Linda Srere, Board Director,   159
Electronic Arts, Inc., Universal Technical
Institute, Inc., and aQuantive, Inc.

Denise Morrison, President,   163
Campbell USA

Stephanie Burns, President & CEO,   167
Dow Corning Corporation

Miriam Vializ-Briggs, Vice President,   171
Marketing, IBM,
Systems & Technology Group

Shaunna Sowell, Vice President,   175
Manager, DFAB, Texas Instruments

Joyce Roché, President & CEO,   179
Girls Inc.

Judith Shapiro, President,   183
Barnard College

Appendix   187

Index   195

About the Author   199

ACKNOWLEDGMENTS

Special thanks to Molly Lepeska, Mindy Meyers, Angela Kim, Gina Carey, Julia Baxter, Jennifer Coffey, Meredith Deliso, Lisette Johnson, Nicole Ferraro and Marilyn Mead. I appreciate the support of my editor, Donya Dickerson, and editing supervisor, Daina Penikas, as well as Ellen Griffith, Suzanne Danielle, and Marjorie Vincent.

It's Time for You to Take Smart Risks

Men have traditionally held the reins on economic power. They've been in the public sphere longer than we have, but we are catching up—achieving greater professional success than ever before. According to calculations by the National Women's Business Council, women start 424 new enterprises every day, more than two times the rate for all U.S. firms.[1] According to 2005 data gathered by the Bureau of Labor Statistics, women hold roughly 50 percent of managerial positions.[2] Even though we comprise half of all management, professional, and related occupations, only 15.7 percent of corporate officers in Fortune 500 companies are women.[3] Further, only 13.6 percent of Fortune 500 board seats are held by women (lots more work to do to level the playing field).[4]

We have the power to overcome obstacles in our paths and create positive change. One way of doing this is to take Smart Risks. Throughout this book you will meet women who have stepped out of their comfort zones and taken leaps. Despite their

---

[1] Calculations by the National Women's Business Council, using data fron the U.S. Census Bureau and the Center for Women's Business Research.

[2] Bureau of Labor Statistics, Current Population Survey, unpublished data, 2005.

[3] Catalyst, 2002 *Catalyst Census of Women Corporate Officers and Top Earners.*

[4] Catalyst, 2003 *Catalyst Census of Women Board Directors.*

fears, they've moved ahead with faith, confident that whatever the outcome, they could handle it. Isn't it time for you to do this too?

Is there an area in your life where you feel stagnant? Too afraid to venture out and try something new? Don't you deserve more? You are about to be given a program to help you take a Smart Risk. Read on to find out how to choose the right one!

PREFACE:
LIVE IN THE LEAP

*Know what the landing strip looks like; set a goal and get clear
on your intention; get a mentor so you can avoid mistakes others
have made; create a financial safety net—a contingency plan—
and trust your instincts.*

—Sue Taigman, Founder,
Clear Choice Coaching and Mediation

We know that the path to becoming successful in business
involves taking some risks, yet many of us are afraid to do this.
Why is that? For one thing, risk-taking removes us from our
comfort zone. It could feel like you are about to jump off a cliff,
with no safety net below. No wonder you feel safer where you
are. But every time we opt for security rather than trying something new, we lose a bit of our excitement for life.

With the program I've developed, you will not be asked to
take just any risk. In this book, I will encourage you to face your
fear when situations line up for you to risk and advance. From
first-hand experience I've created six steps that have helped me
move forward in my career and can be used by you too.

My decision to leave a lucrative job felt like a frightening leap at times, but turned out to be a Smart Risk that paid off. Eighteen years ago, I found myself in a rut, working as a marketing executive for a large newspaper. I envisioned moving on and creating television programs about health and empowerment issues that would support women. Although I had outgrown the job, I was making a good salary with benefits and a pension. I couldn't get up the nerve to quit. Most people thought I was crazy even to contemplate switching careers. Their concerns only made me more nervous about taking a risk. At the same time, the thought of a change excited me.

The turning point came for me when the discomfort of staying in a rut—going to work every day when I had lost my enthusiasm for my job—became unbearable. Starting my own company began to seem like a viable option. I had told my employer that I was going to return at the end of my maternity leave. After the birth of my son, I decided to report back to work. But the second I walked into the building, I knew I couldn't go back. I went into my boss's office and resigned. My breathing was irregular, and I was a bundle of nerves on the inside for weeks. Although I was excited, the fear of being out there alone, without a Fortune 500 company behind me, seemed overwhelming. But I did it! I took a step toward my goal. My passion to make a difference was greater than any fears I had. In fact, I realized I was more excited than afraid!

In addition to my job at the newspaper, I had written books on weight loss and embracing change. After having maintained a

50-pound weight loss for a great many years, I wanted to share the strategies that had worked for me with other people. I was a natural coach and had been a great guest on talk shows. Looking to expand these talents, I decided that now was the time to have my own program and provide women across the globe with the mentoring I had given friends and colleagues. But then doubts crept in. Could I really live my vision and get paid well for it? If it took too long for the business to turn a profit, could I survive on my savings?

Since my skills were in sales and marketing, I needed to get some television production experience. With my infant son strapped to my chest, I walked into a major video arts trade school and made a deal: I would help them market their school if they would let me take the classes I needed. I took everything I could: editing, TV writing, production. I eventually met with the head of a major medical institution in New York, convinced him to give me a small budget, and with that I created my first program. The institution became my first sponsor. Fifteen years later, my company does amazing and powerful work. Our award-winning television shows appear on public television stations across the country, and we recently won our second Emmy. Our Web site, www.womenworking.com, is considered a source of inspiration and information by working women around the globe.

I breathe peacefully now. I head a thriving business doing what I love. Each day is a new adventure—not always an easy one, but one that is different and challenging. None of this would have happened, however, if I hadn't taken a Smart Risk. Through my work, I'm in touch with many women who could benefit from risk-taking. They want to loosen the grip of jobs, habits, and people they've outgrown, but they haven't yet and need support to do so.

Women from our member network at womenworking.com shed some light on this issue. Based on the results of an informal risk-taking survey, members who responded felt that women had a slightly harder time than men when it came to initiating big changes and taking risks. Over 67 percent believed that when growing up, women are encouraged to be agreeable and submissive rather than assertive and take action. In addition, over 40 percent felt that women have too many people depending on them to take uncertain actions. As Shelley Treacy of Microsoft's Real Time Collaboration Group told us, "Women unfortunately are still socialized to be accommodating and think of others first, yet are more resourceful and better suited to take risks than men. We unfortunately have not been rewarded in our careers for the skills that are required to be successful risk-takers."

One of the respondents to our Risk-Taking Survey, Melissa Cline, fought her tendency to put others first, and made the transition from purchasing to human resources at her company. She says, "I learned that it's okay to take a risk and focus on myself and what I wanted to do. I had been so worried about the impacts to my current department that I hesitated to do what was best for me."

Although 68 percent of the respondents were generally satisfied with their current careers, the ones that weren't cited the following as their main reasons for dissatisfaction:

- Other passions that are more compelling (43.6 percent)
- Lack of upward mobility (43 percent)
- A feeling of stagnation (38.4 percent)
- Being overworked, not enough time for family and friends (34.3 percent)
- Inadequate monetary compensation (32.6 percent)

Over 38 percent were working to change their current situations, and over 35 percent thought they might be looking to make a change in the future. Many women viewed taking risks as a way to do this—and risks may come more naturally than you think.

Your Turn

I would be willing to bet that, years ago, you were quite the risk-taker. Think back to when you were a child. You would probably do anything, eat anything, run circles around the playground for hours, and dive after a ball as if you were invincible. Nothing held you back. You had no problem taking risks.

In fact, children are natural risk-takers. They are powerful because they believe they have a right to succeed and are unwilling to accept the limitations that grown-ups see as their reality. Several years ago, while walking down the road, my son and I were stopped by three 6-year-old girls who were selling their old toys. They had faith that people would buy their tattered teddy bears and took the risk to set up shop near a small park. I gave my son a dollar and encouraged him to pick out one of the stuffed animals. As we were about to leave, I told the girls to keep up the good work and walked away smiling. I had the feeling that I would be reading about one or all of them in the future. Who knows, maybe they'll be CEOs of corporations in the year 2040!

As we age, we lose that sense of entitlement and confidence. Instead, we follow the path we believe is safe, hoping to provide for our families and find a job we're satisfied with. We stop taking risks because we equate them with danger rather than with opportunity. Imagine what would happen if you could move forward confidently without the fear of failure overpowering you. With my program, your fear may be there but you'll be encouraged to take a Smart Risk anyway.

In truth, we take risks every day. They're not the exception but the norm. Everything we do involves a certain amount of risk, from taking our children to school to going to the post office. Each time you leave your home something unforeseen could happen. There are no guarantees that it won't. But we do these things nevertheless.

In this book I will talk about taking strategic risks—risks born out of thought and intuition. You will be given six steps to determine the right risk to take regarding a business goal. Why stay stuck because you might be afraid? You have too much to accomplish.

In Step One, you will commit to this goal. You won't be asked to risk blindly, but rather encouraged to take action when circumstances line up.

Successful people take Smart Risks, but only with their eyes wide open. I am not asking you to jump into a pool with no water.

I will offer a Risk Quotient in Step Two. Through a method of weighing consequences, you can determine if your actions are likely to be successful (a Best Bet), if they have possibility for a future time (a Not Now), or if they're likely to fail (a No Go). Best Bets should be taken immediately and Not Nows revisited at a later time.

All research points to the fact that support is one of the most powerful tools you'll need to create change. Step Three guides you through the process of getting support from the appropriate people. Winners form alliances and rely on feedback to help them benchmark with colleagues as they take action.

When you have identified a Smart Risk, it's important to follow through. Step Four gives you strategies to make sure that procrastination, perfectionism, and second-guessing do not get in the way of victory. Here, you will plan your leap and not look back.

You've taken action and are on your way to achieving your goal. Savor that sweet taste of success! In Step Five, you'll be encouraged to brag. Claim your accomplishments and let everyone know. As women, we sometimes have a hard time doing that. Many of us have been taught to be humble and modest and to resist speaking about our achievements in a boastful way. It's important to recognize that the more you vocalize your success, the more confident you'll become. Also, your example can be inspirational to others who may be stuck on Step One.

Step Six encourages you to keep going and to take personal inspiration from your own story. The last hindrance you face is the Plateau Mentality. It is easy to bask in your victory and not take further action. I will encourage you to keep the memory of your success green and apply these risk-taking principles to other areas of your life.

Finally, in Part Two, you'll be inspired by women who have calculated their next steps, looked fear in the face, and taken the leap. Their experiences will support you in your own risk-taking process. Although several of these pioneers may be at the top of their careers, they continue to set goals and take Smart Risks much in the same way that you are doing right now. With a plan and these six action steps, you too will be propelled to a new level. Let's get started.

PART ONE

FOLLOW
THE
SIX-STEP PROGRAM

STEP ONE

COMMIT TO YOUR GOAL

DECLARATION:

I am open to new beginnings and will declare a goal
that stretches my abilities further and takes me to
the next level.

QUALITIES OF A SMART RISK-TAKER:

Awareness

Clarity

Focus

If you have a bigger plan for yourself, then keep that goal in mind. Every day is a step toward your big goal. Your life should be limitless. When you limit yourself, you go nowhere.

—Jess Alpert Goldman,
Founder of World According to Jess

You deserve more. You will never stop growing in your career so long as you keep reaching higher. Being complacent means settling for less, and you don't want to do that. Listen to that yearning deep inside you—to be more, to exercise your potential. Whether personal, social, or professional, you need to continually set new goals for yourself.

In this chapter, you will focus on selecting a work-related goal that involves a certain amount of risk. You may already have a goal in mind, and if that's the case, great! The chapter ahead will help you define it more clearly. If you do not have a goal or are unsure of which one to choose, we will help you focus on choosing the right one to explore.

Choose a Goal You Feel Passionate About!

What makes you excited and gets the blood racing in your veins? It could be something you've wanted to do but have been putting on the back burner because of other obligations. Handling day-to-day tasks often leaves us with little time for reflection, causing us to end up stuck in situations that we've outgrown. You may deny that there's something greater for you to shoot for. That's not true—there is. Barbara Cowden, Executive Vice President at State Farm advises, "Look to align your talents with what you are doing. Passion is a great motivator. If you are not making headway, a change may be in order."

The goal you identify could transition you to a new career or catapult your advancement at your current job. Do you deserve a raise or a promotion? Do you want to move to another division in your company? Do you want to change professions? Whatever your goal is, you must be passionate about it and feel that it is really worth pursuing. Those steps that seem risky may in fact be the risk-key to opening up new opportunities for yourself.

When I took a leap, I had to build up my confidence to do it. I wanted to create television programs that would make a difference in women's lives. As I mentioned in the preface, I was working for a newspaper and earning a good salary at the time, but I had outgrown my job. The thought that I could actually set a new target for myself was exhilarating. I didn't know how it would all happen, but I was committed to taking action to move it along. I felt a bit overwhelmed, but I realized that I only had to take one step at a time. When I broke my goal up into a series of doable actions, I could go forward with conviction. In this chapter you'll be asked to reflect on and answer many questions. Take this seriously because it will lead you to select the right goal for yourself.

Let's begin by setting an enthusiastic tone. Think about what brings you satisfaction and joy. These things can be totally unrelated. For me, I love to act, adore flowers, and take great satisfaction when I see others succeed at new ventures. Now that I have my own business, I incorporate my acting skills in the television programs I host and produce, fill my office with fresh flowers weekly, and create empowering media to help our audiences advance in their lives. Though flowers and acting may seem unrelated, acknowledging the things I love helped me shape my career path and create a business that is flourishing. While most of the women who responded to our Risk-Taking Survey were generally pleased with their careers, those who weren't reported having other passions that were more compelling. Identifying what you are passionate about will help you select the right goal—a goal that's highly charged.

What sparks your interest these days? Write that down below. If you hit a blank, think of a time when you were younger. What hobbies did you pursue? What activities did you look forward to doing?

My Interests:

- _____
  _____
  _____
- _____
  _____
  _____

- _____
  _____
  _____
  _____

Keep your interests in mind when committing to a goal at the end of this chapter. You want to work toward something that keeps you engaged and comes to fruition.

───────── *TRAILBLAZER* ─────────
Ellen Ochoa (1958–present)
A research engineer when she was selected by NASA to join its astronaut program, Ellen became the first Hispanic woman in space in April 1993. She returned to space in 1994 and again in 1999 as a member of the Discovery crew that executed the first docking to the International Space Station.

Next, it's useful to remember when you've taken successful risks. Call upon memories of doing something daring, no matter how insignificant the incident might seem. When did you take a risk in your personal or work life and get the results you wanted? For example, did you ask for a raise and get one? Did you approach someone reading a book you wanted to buy and strike up a conversation that started a friendship?

Recalling past times when you took a leap sets up a positive framework for moving forward. Affirm two situations:

Situation One:

I took a risk by: _____

_____

_____

How it turned out: _____

_____

_____

Situation Two:

I took a risk by: _____

_____

_____

How it turned out: _____

_____

_____

The Fear Factor

What inhibits you from moving forward? When you identify a goal and take actions to achieve it, you open up yourself to the possibility of risk—getting or not getting what you desire, as well as the consequences that result. It's frightening to step outside your comfort zone, which is what you are doing when you take a risk. You'll likely be afraid, but that doesn't have to stop you from taking action. As Susan Jeffers, author of *Feel the Fear and Do It*

Anyway says, "As long as I continued to push out into the world, as long as I continued to stretch my capabilities, as long as I continued to take new risks in making my dreams come true, I was going to experience fear."

—————————— *TRAILBLAZER* ——————————

Muriel Siebert (1932–present)

Muriel came to New York in 1954 and was hired as a research analyst on Wall Street. Thirteen years later, she became the first woman to occupy a seat on the New York Stock Exchange.

Insurance employee Gayle Wolschlag was afraid to transition from the comfort of her job at a small company to take on more responsibility at a national corporation. She says, "I had gained respect, a good position, had a job that I loved and could do in my sleep." She knew she would be trading a sense of security for the unknown, but she also realized that it was the perfect time to take a leap—and she did. Today, her new position offers her a higher salary, bonuses, and more opportunity for job mobility.

Gayle didn't allow her fear to paralyze her. As the wise acronym suggests, FEAR is just False Evidence Appearing Real. What's the worst that could happen if your goal doesn't work out? You'll still be a winner because you've tried something new. As the saying goes, if you shoot for the moon and miss, you'll still be among the stars. Lani Guinier, author, former civil rights attorney, and the first woman of color to join the tenured faculty at Harvard Law School, has what she calls a "failure theory of success." In a University of Illinois commencement address, she stated: "Failure can also push us to innovate—to experiment—to move forward with new ideas. That is one of the great things about the American dream. It encourages us to be entrepreneurial—to be innovative. It pushes us to take risks, to dare to be powerful in the service of our vision." Do you think the possibility of failure is worse than staying stuck in a rut or not exploring your potential? Well, it isn't. It's more debilitating to see a friend or colleague accomplish something you could have done. *Now* is the time to take action.

Turn Fear into Excitement

I invite you to shift how you view fear. Did you ever think that when you're afraid, you are actually excited? Our bodies react to fear and excitement in the same way——a quickened heartbeat, perspiration, cold and clammy hands. I remember how I worried after I received a promotion at my first job. I was concerned about my new responsibilities and whether I could handle them. My mentor advised me that I wouldn't have been offered the position if others didn't think I could do it, and do it well. She also pointed out that it sounded like I was more excited than afraid. Suddenly, my attitude changed. Her guidance and friendship gave me the permission I needed to feel exhilarated about my new job. Consequently, I was looking forward to moving ahead.

Take one of your daring situations from the earlier exercise and see if your fear masked your excitement about trying something new. Answer the following questions to become clear on what actually happened.

I took a risk by: _____

_____

_____

_____

_____

Was I aware of any physical sensations as I took action?

_____

_____

_____

_____

What was I telling myself as it was happening (negative/positive thoughts)? _____

_____

_____

_____

_____

Did I feel fear, excitement, or both? _____

_____

_____

_____

At the time, did you let yourself get excited about trying something new, or were you too afraid? If the latter was the case, can you see how you were choosing to focus on the fear, and not on the fact that you were embarking on something new? If you change how you think about a situation, you'll change how you experience it. Take this example:

Kelly had always wanted to be a graphic artist. Her art teachers praised her talent throughout school, but she didn't get much encouragement at home. Growing up, she was responsible for taking care of her brothers and sisters while both her parents worked, and her own interests were put aside. After graduating from a community college, she worked for a small company as an administrative assistant. She did her job well, but was looking to do more. At one point, there was a need for someone to design a brochure. Kelly volunteered, and her brochure was so good that coworkers began to ask her to design presentations for them. After a year, she was eligible for the company tuition reimbursement program, and she decided to take an advanced course in design at a technical school. She didn't expect to be as anxious as she was when she enrolled, but a talk with a friend helped her focus on the fact that she would be developing her talent in a field she loved. She went from feeling scared and anxious to motivated and excited. Kelly still had some trepidation, but was now looking forward to the class.

You too can turn your fear into excitement. New challenges are scary—and exhilarating. Know this: You have the skills, or can acquire the necessary skills, to meet any challenge. Right now, I want you to change your mindset about risk-taking. Know that you take risks all the time. You don't do it occasionally. Own that! Just walking outside your home in the morning, for example. Crossing the street. Trying a new restaurant. So what about thinking, *"I'm ready to up the ante—to be more open to taking Smart Risks that advance my career and my life."*

TRAILBLAZER

Ellen Swallow Richards (1842–1911)

Following her graduation from Vassar College, Ellen applied to and was accepted at MIT, becoming the first woman admitted to the university. She graduated in 1873 and went on to become the first professional female chemist in the United States.

I want you to consider a business goal you've been afraid to tackle, one that will propel you forward. It may or may not be the one you select to use with our Six-Step Program, but for now, examine why you haven't yet taken action on it. For example, maybe it hasn't been the right time. Maybe you lack the confidence to think you can make it happen, or, out of fear, you stay vague about what the next steps might be.

There are an infinite number of ways that our goals get tabled, or worse, forgotten, as we deal with the daily challenges and stressors life hands us. There will be distractions along the way and seemingly good reasons why you can't achieve a goal. You may have been promised a promotion that never came through and you are frustrated about going after another position. It may be that you have been asking the wrong people for advice—people who don't have your best interest at heart. And you listen to them.

TRAILBLAZER

Kathrine Switzer

At just 20 years old, Kathrine became the first woman to enter and run the Boston Marathon. During the 1967 race, the race director, upset that a female was participating in the traditionally all-male event, tried to remove her from the track. She didn't let him stop her and continued running in marathons across the globe.

Whatever the case, you must become aware of your own defeatist thoughts so that you don't indulge them. They will deter you from taking action or going beyond what you know. To achieve your goals, you need to focus on what's positive. You need to replace negative mind-talk with affirming thoughts. Refer to the chart Examining Mind-Talk on the next page for some examples of pessimistic thinking that keeps you stuck versus mind-talk that gets you moving.

EXAMINING MIND-TALK

MIND-TALK THAT KEEPS YOU STUCK	MIND-TALK THAT MOVES YOU FORWARD
I can't do something different. I have too many people who depend on me. What if I fail?	The people in my life want me to succeed and will support me to try something new.
I'm too _____ (old, uneducated, etc.—fill in the blank) to transition into something new.	Grandma Moses and Georgia O'Keeffe painted well into their senior years with acclaim. I have a wealth of experiences to bring to any new situation.
I'm not going to achieve what I want, why even try?	I have clarity about what I want and I'm going to achieve it. I can reach out for support along the way.
I can't afford to launch out in a new way.	If all I am is financially secure but I stop growing, how happy will I actually be?
I've failed before. What makes me think this time it will be different?	There is no such thing as failure if I learn from each experience. Why not attempt something new?

Songwriter and metaphysical teacher, David Friedman, defines the process of finding positive replacement phrases as a *thought exchange*. You just have to be honest with yourself, spot your negative thought and replace it with a positive phrase that is charged with meaning for you. For example, if deep down you think that you can only go so far in your career, you will manifest just that. Why not exchange your thought for, "There are a world of opportunities open to me at work."

What are the thoughts you've been holding that are limiting your advancing on-the-job? Reflect on this, then write them down below.

I hold myself back by thinking:

1. _____
_____
_____
_____

2. _____
_____
_____
_____

3. _____
_____
_____
_____

Whatever you've just written, it's time to move on. I want you to replace those thoughts with affirming ones.

I will move myself forward by thinking:

1. _____
_____

2. _____
_____
_____
_____
_____

3. _____
_____
_____
_____

This new way of thinking will help you achieve your goal. It will make you feel more confident, and that will boost your ability. Take note of when you think negatively as you go about your tasks during the day. When you become aware, stop what you are doing. You must discipline yourself to replace these thoughts with positive ones. This is a powerful strategy used by Smart Risk-Takers. If the grip of a debilitating habit is strong, call upon a supportive friend to help you get back on track.

Time to Commit

You're about to select a goal that you will explore further in Step Two. It doesn't have to be one that will launch a new career, but it can be. It may be a step you've wanted to take at your current job but haven't yet. Keep in mind that goal-setting is just the beginning. Smart Risk-Taking is a process that happens over time and involves perseverance. You are about to commit to making the first move as Abby, an acquaintance of mine, did.

Abby had been a beauty consultant for 10 years. Her job no longer presented her with new challenges. When I asked her what she wanted to do next, she skirted the question and said she didn't really know. "Yes, you do know," I said, "but you're afraid to voice it." Through my encouragement, she searched further. "You're right. I want to write," she said. "In fact, there's a screenwriting course being offered at the local college this summer, right near the salon. I think it would be hilarious to write a movie about the beauty business." When I told her, "Take the course," she smiled and said she would register.

Ultimately, Abby wanted to be a screenwriter and took a conservative step toward achieving that goal. She didn't quit her job, fly to Hollywood, and set her laptop down outside of a movie studio. Taking those actions would have been too severe. If they didn't work out, the risk would be financially depleting and self-defeating.

━━━━━━━━━ *TRAILBLAZER* ━━━━━━━━━

Lucille Ball (1911–1989)

A successful and beloved television comedienne, film actress, and independent TV producer, Lucille Ball transformed live television comedy during the medium's formative years. Her top-rated show, I Love Lucy, *first entered the hearts and living rooms of viewers nationwide in the 1950s. Thank you, Lucy, for your silly antics, perfect comedic timing, and ditzy charm.*

Some of us purposely name an impossible task, set out to attain it, and say, "I knew I couldn't do it," when we fail. Then we can claim that we took a risk that didn't work and place the blame for our unhappiness somewhere other than on ourselves. Why set yourself up for failure like that? That's not to say that you can't dream big; you just have to set a realistic plan to attain your goal.

Carla Cooper, Senior Vice President at PepsiCo, believes that, for women, goal-setting is particularly challenging because of a lack of corporate female role models and a mistaken, widespread belief that high-level success is unattainable. She notes, "If you don't believe that you are qualified for a high-level position, or that it isn't possible for you and others like you to get those jobs, you're probably not going to make it to the top." She believes the solution lies in "knowing and feeling confident that anything is possible, because it is. It's when we set our goals below our capabilities that we fall short of the big, high-impact power positions."

Make your goal something attainable, but don't be afraid to go the distance to get what you really want. As Smart Risk-Takers, we are climbing a ladder step by step. Each successful step will be motivation to pursue the next one. Start out by taking just one action toward your goal, like Abby's screenwriting course. Here's another example, if you want to become an entertainment lawyer, your strategy should be as follows: *I want to go to law school and get the credentials I need. Right now I'll take the LSAT so I can apply to schools by the end of the year. (First action: Law School Exam.)*

The questions below will help you identify a goal you'll follow using our Six-Step Program. Take time to think about your responses before writing them down. Some of the questions may not apply to you, but don't dismiss them without reflection:

What have I outgrown in my current job? _____

_____

_____

_____

_____

Why have I stayed with something that may not be right for me anymore? _____

_____

_____

_____

_____

Can I alter my current situation and make it a growth opportunity? If so, how? _____

_____

_____

_____

_____

What job would I like to ultimately see myself doing?

_____

_____

_____

_____

Do I need to change my company, or career? _____

_____

_____

_____

_____

Has a goal become clear? If not, focus on an action you can take to make your current situation more dynamic. For example, if you see a growth opportunity at your company that interests you, your goal is to put your best effort forward to get that job. If that is not an option for you and you need to change companies/industries, think about what type of organization you would like to be affiliated with. Say you are selling mainframe computers, but would ultimately like to sell advertising space for a magazine—then the latter is your goal. If you know you want to change careers altogether, now or in the future, then Lauren's example may be helpful.

Lauren is a copywriter for a large public relations agency. She's great at what she does, but her job doesn't satisfy her creative yearnings. She adores gardening and flowers. When you walk into her home, her floral arrangements are everywhere. It's clear that floral design is her passion.

She's exploring careers that would allow her to remain financially secure, but also fuel her creativity. Her passion is clear and she will use it as the basis for developing goals she can possibly work toward. Here is Lauren's Career-Vision list, ideal professional options that she may want to pursue.

- Open up my own flower shop
- Create specialty products, (e.g., cards using floral essences)
- Design women's scarves and sell them to department stores
- Work at a botanical garden
- Write for a home and garden magazine
- Go back to school and become a landscaper

TRAILBLAZER

Anita Roddick (1942–present)

The Body Shop is a global business known for its innovative products, as well as its activism, but its beginnings nearly 30 years ago were decidedly more modest. Anita founded the company with no experience or training to support herself and her two daughters while her husband was abroad.

Filling out a Career-Vision list can help you focus your options to explore a new career, as Lauren is doing; to change companies or industries; or to advance at your current job, as Beth is considering. She's an assistant editor at a business magazine, and knows she wants to move up the ranks in publishing. The options on her Career-Vision list are to seek a promotion as an editor where she is, switch to another magazine at her company, or go back to school and earn a higher degree while still working.

Write down a list of your possible Career Visions:

My Career-Vision List

- _____
  _____
  _____
  _____
  _____

- _____
  _____
  _____
  _____
  _____

- _____
  _____
  _____
  _____

- _____
  _____
  _____
  _____

- _____
  _____
  _____

_____

_____

_____

Now it's time to prioritize your Career Visions using the Benefit Evaluation Method. Look at your list and choose the three Career Visions that most excite you. To help you decide which one of these three Career Visions to choose as a goal, you'll need to reflect on what benefits you want to get by moving forward. Do you want to earn as much or more money than you are currently earning? Have more time off to spend with your family? Travel the world? Work from your home? If you are having trouble narrowing in on these, think about what you want to improve about your current job and how making a change would affect that. Lauren did this in her inventory chart.

LAUREN'S INVENTORY

LIMITATIONS OF LAUREN'S CURRENT JOB	BENEFITS SHE WANTS MOVING FORWARD
Work is not stimulating	Use my creativity more
Low salary	Pay raise
Involved in too many group projects	Work independently
Long hours	Allow more time to spend with family
Few breaks during the workday	Have some downtime

Now, list what you don't like about your existing situation and what benefits you would want going forward. Fill out your own inventory chart.

YOUR INVENTORY

LIMITATIONS OF YOUR CURRENT JOB	BENEFITS YOU WANT MOVING FORWARD

In advancing her career, Lauren felt certain benefits were more important than others and ranked them in the following way, using a scale of 1 (not important) to 5 (extremely important).

Take a look at what Lauren's Benefit Evaluation Table looks like on the next page:

LAUREN'S BENEFIT EVALUATION TABLE

	Use of Creativity	Increase Income	Work Independently	Spend more time w/family	Get out of office more
Weight of Importance	4	3	1	2	2

Next, she took this process one step further, looked at her top three career moves, and evaluated their benefits accordingly using the 1–5 scale.

LAUREN'S TOP THREE CAREER VISIONS ➤ ➤ ➤

BENEFITS ▼ ▼ ▼	Write for Home/ Garden Magazine	Start own line of floral-inspired products	Go back to school and become a landscaper
Use creativity in work	3	4	1
Increase income	0	2	0
Work inde-pendently	2	1	1
Spend more time with family	0	2	2
Get out of office more	3	2	2
Total	**8**	**11**	**6**

Throughout this process, she kept in mind what benefits she valued most. Lauren determined that starting her own floral-inspired product line best met her needs.

Which of your top three Career Visions offers you the most? Fill out the charts that follow to find out.

First list, then rank the benefits that are important to you in advancing your career, using a scale of 1(not important) to 5 (extremely important).

YOUR BENEFIT EVALUATION TABLE

	Benefit #1	Benefit #2	Benefit #3	Benefit #4	Benefit #5
	____	____	____	____	____
Weight of Importance					

Next, look at your top three Career Visions and evaluate how each benefit is fulfilled by a particular option.

This chart will reveal helpful insights, but keep in mind what benefits you value most when determining what option is best for you. You can choose to use this as the goal you'll be exploring in our Six-Step Program.

YOUR TOP THREE CAREER VISIONS ➤ ➤ ➤

BENEFITS ▼ ▼ ▼			
Total			

Your Six-Step Program Goal

Whether your goal involves changing careers or companies, or staying where you are and advancing, you are ready to declare a goal now. Review the exercises that helped define what you want, then commit to a goal by writing it down on the next page.

My Goal:

_____

_____

_____

_____

_____

Congratulations! You've taken the first step in our Smart Risk Program. In the next chapter, you'll find out if pursuing your goal is a Best Bet.

Coming up: the Risk Quotient.

Quick Tips

- Get confident! Reach into your memory bank—think of the times when you've taken a leap and succeeded (no matter how small it was).
- Get honest! What are the thoughts you hold that are limiting you? Awareness is key. Exchange them for more positive ones.
- Get passionate! Choose a goal that you care about. This will motivate you to persevere and follow-through when the going gets tough, and it will.

POWER LINK: For inspirational stories of women who have successfully aligned their passions with their work, visit www.womenworking.com/feature

STEP TWO

CALCULATE — DETERMINE YOUR RISK QUOTIENT

DECLARATION:

I use my mental and intuitive abilities to determine whether my goal is a Best Bet. If it is, I move forward with courage and tenacity.

QUALITIES OF A SMART RISK-TAKER:

Honesty

Resolve

Insight

When I choose to take a risk, I follow a strategy that is one-third wisdom and insights from others and two-thirds heart, using feelings and intuition.

—Gail Sussman Miller,
Coach and Speaker, Inspired Choice

Imagine that you are in a familiar room with the lights off. Although ordinarily you know your way around, the darkness makes it difficult to navigate and to find your way out. You take a deep breath, blink your eyes, and rely on memory, logic, and intuition to chart a path to the door that marks your exit. Maneuvering through a somewhat uncertain path using both your head and your heart for guidance is the key to advancing. Through calculated steps based on logic and trust, you are able to seize the opportunity on the other side of the door.

Accomplished people take Smart Risks by analyzing the possible outcomes of their actions, looking at the timing of a goal, weighing it with their other priorities, and trusting their intuition about the "rightness" of taking the risk. When these factors line up in a positive way, successful people take what I call a Best Bet.

Later on in this chapter, you will be introduced to the Risk Quotient I've developed. By using it you will be able to decide whether you should take the risk you're considering. If it is one to pursue, you will be encouraged to face your fear about moving forward and take action. When you do, your fears will take a backseat to the excitement of taking on a new challenge.

A while ago, I saw a television program about outrageous weddings. One of the couples actually exchanged their vows on a bridge high above a river—a natural choice for them, as they were going to bungee jump right afterwards. As they said their "I Dos," the newlyweds leapt, with their relatives cheering them on as they took their "wedding dive." The exhilaration that they felt as they jumped is what I feel when I am about to take a risk and it looks like I will succeed. However, my excitement is sometimes coupled with discomfort.

Although I am anticipating a positive outcome, my instinctual fear cautions me not to move ahead. Yet it's not the risk itself that is creating the problem, but the *fear* of leaving my comfort zone. In order to push forward, I decide to act only on a plan that is calculated and well thought out. So I take a deep breath and place my trust in simple logic. Supportive friends and colleagues, much like the cheering wedding guests, encourage me when I'm about to try something new. Their words and gestures cushion my leap as I jump. I allow myself to feel excited about the prospects before me.

What Is a Smart Risk?

It may or may not be in your best interest to pursue a goal you've identified. As we proceed, it is important to understand a few definitions:

- **Best Bet:** A risk that's worth taking
- **No Go:** A risk that will probably fail
- **Not Now:** A risk that is not worth taking now, but should be revisited in the future

―――――――――――― *TRAILBLAZER* ――――――――――――
Victoria Claflin Woodhull (1838–1927)

In 1871, Victoria became one of the first women to speak in front of a Congressional panel when she lobbied for women's right to vote. She later inspired a generation of suffragettes as America's first female presidential candidate. Though her 1872 presidential bid under the Equal Rights Party failed, she continued to venture out in other areas.

Throughout this chapter, I'll be using examples of women who have successfully taken risks. As you read on, keep in mind the goal you identified in Step One. You'll find out if it's worth pursuing. Remember that there is no sure thing, but there are Best Bets—that's the whole point of using the Risk Quotient.

Establish the Mindset

Before making the calculations needed to determine the projected success of taking an action, you must put yourself in the mindset to move forward. Whereas risk-taking is much like bungee jumping in its emotional entanglement of exhilaration and fear, the personal qualities of individuals who assume these roles differ dramatically. Many bungee jumpers are thrill-seekers, often driven by spontaneity; successful risk-takers are individuals who act upon careful deliberation.

The Risk Quotient I offer allows you to unite caution with ambition. Hence, do not dismiss the advice of this book because of misperceptions about the type of people who take risks. Smart Risk-Takers evaluate decisions before they leap.

Researching your move is essential, so learn all you can. In our Risk-Taking Survey, over 84 percent of our respondents thought that "planning" was crucial before making a big change. Study the industry you're interested in, network with people that excel in jobs you'd like to do someday. Find out what their career paths were.

According to Catalyst, a leading research and advisory organization to businesses, 40 percent of women in corporate leadership positions said that "seeking out difficult or highly visible assignments" was a very important strategy for advancement.[1] These projects involve risk, and could place careers on the fast track.

The Risk Quotient

The Risk Quotient is made up of three parts:
1.   Analyzing the pros and cons of taking a risk,
2.   Considering timing and your other priorities,
3.   And, most importantly, listening to your gut sense.

[1] Catalyst, *Women in U.S. Corporate Leadership: 2003*, page 13.

Part One: Pros and Cons

What are the pros and cons of taking the risk?

This is where you let logic rule, where you'll assess the consequences of taking an action.

To begin calculating your Risk Quotient, you will make a simple list of the pluses and minuses. Most of us do this already. Here's how Karen applied the Risk Quotient to determine if she'd take a job requiring a new skill set. She had outgrown her marketing position and was considering changing functions—she thought she'd make a first-rate saleswoman. A position opened up with one of her company's overseas start-up ventures. They were willing to train the right people. Karen was intrigued by the prospect of transitioning from marketing to sales.

Here was her list of pros and cons to decide whether she'd apply for the opportunity.

The Risk: To join a team as one of the 20 salespeople opening the Brussels office.

Pros

- Receive sales training and break into a new career.
- The new office is a "hot" project—the likelihood of success is strong. Meet new people and experience a different culture.
- Gain visibility if the division does well—may lead to a promotion.
- No real downside if the division fails, I'm one of 20.

- Make more money—bonus structure of a sales job as opposed to a marketing position.

- Company will find me housing.

Cons

- The differences in cultures might be difficult to navigate.

- I will be away from friends and family—could be isolating.

- I don't have a steady boyfriend and want to date, which may be difficult. I want to start a family in the next few years.

- As an outsider, I may not be respected by some of my colleagues who are native to the country.

- Cost of living is higher than where I am now.

Before you tabulate the pluses and the minuses of a goal, you'll need to consider the weight of each item in both columns. This portion will require some thinking, because no one can tell you how much each plus or minus means to you. Some people dislike being alone and may seriously consider the isolation factor to outweigh most of the pluses. Alternatively, others may enjoy time alone, considering it a period of rejuvenation rather than isolation. Establish a scale of 1 (not important) to 5 (extremely important), and attach a numerical value to each plus and minus. This way, the Risk Quotient has become individualized, tailored to suit your personal needs. Karen's pluses and minuses are listed in Karen's Risk Quotient Balance Sheet along with her numeric ratings.

KAREN'S RISK QUOTIENT BALANCE SHEET

➕	➖
I'm excited by the opportunity to receive sales training and break into a sales career. **Rated: (3)**	The differences in cultures might be hard to navigate. **Rated: (1)**
My company has done preliminary research. The new office is one of their "hot" projects—the likelihood of success is strong. **Rated: (2)**	I will be away from friends and family—may feel isolated. **Rated: (2)**
I'll be able to meet new people and broaden my horizons by living in a different culture. **Rated: (4)**	I don't have a steady boyfriend and want to date. I'd like to start a family in the next few years. There may be little opportunity to meet men. **Rated: (4)**
I'd gain high visibility in my company if the division does well—may lead to a promotion. **Rated: (5)**	It may be hard to gain respect as an outsider from some of my colleagues who are native to the country. **Rated: (2)**
There will be no downside if the division fails, I'm one of 20. **Rated: (2)**	Cost of living is higher than where I am now. **Rated: (3)**

(Continued)

(Continued)

+	**−**
The ability to make more money in this job—bonus structure of a sales career as opposed to a marketing job. **Rated: (5)**	
The company will find me housing. **Rated: (1)**	
Total: 22	**Total: 12**

For Karen, "The differences in cultures might be hard to navigate" was attributed a 1, whereas "I'd gain high visibility in my company if the division does well—may lead to a promotion" received a 5. Karen was much more focused on her career at this point in her life and relatively secure in her ability to adapt to a different culture. In fact, she enjoyed traveling, so she attributed little importance to this minus. On the other hand, the possibility that this assignment might skyrocket her career excited her enormously, increasing the weight of the plus. Karen decided that the pluses outweighed the minuses and advanced to the next step. It is also quite possible for the negative factors to predominate and deter you from taking action.

Now tabulate the numerical values attached to the pluses and the minuses of the risk you're evaluating, then review the results. Take time to assess the values of the pluses and minuses of your goal in order to know if you should move on as well.

My Risk: _____

_____

YOUR RISK QUOTIENT BALANCE SHEET

+	−
Total:	**Total:**

Part Two: Timing

Is the timing right?

Timing is everything. When considering whether your risk is a Best Bet, it's important to view it in a larger context. For example, are you just starting your career; are you mid-career; thinking of retirement; or looking to transition into another career or part-time work? Are you single or married? Do you have children? Do you have aging parents? All these factors play an important part in your Risk Quotient.

TRAILBLAZER

Elizabeth Cabot Cary Agassiz (1822–1907)

Elizabeth accompanied her husband, a Swiss naturalist, on research expeditions through Brazil and the Straights of Magellan. In 1879, she helped open the "Harvard Annex" in Cambridge and was appointed president. The school was subsequently named Radcliffe.

Let's look at Karen's situation again. Karen created two timelines in order to evaluate her risk in relation to what life stage she was in. One focused on her career, the other on family. She used arrows to indicate the ideal time to take this risk and where she *actually* was in her life.

Karen's Risk: *Move to Brussels*

CAREER TIMELINE

Ideal time in Karen's life to take the risk

Entry into workforce	**Career peak**	**Retirement**

⇓

⇑

Entry into workforce	**Career peak**	**Retirement**

Actual time in Karen's life

For Karen, the ideal time for a long-distance assignment was when she was starting out, which lined up with where she actually was, so it was a GO.

FAMILY TIMELINE

Ideal time in Karen's life to take the risk

Single	**Married with children**	**Other dependents/ elder parent(s)**

⇓

⇑

Single	**Married with children**	**Other dependents/ elder parent(s)**

Actual time in Karen's life

In terms of family, the ideal situation for a move overseas is when she doesn't have any childcare or eldercare responsibilities. Karen's real situation, once again, aligned with this.

On the other hand, an acquaintance of mine found that her goal was a Not Now because of timing. With two teenagers at home, she had wanted to go back to school and get her MBA. She was working a full-time job, and the added hours needed for study wouldn't allow her to be home much to supervise them. She waited until they were older to pursue her coursework.

What about your risk? Is it the right time for you to take it? Fill out the following timelines and find out.

My Risk: _____

YOUR CAREER TIMELINE

Ideal time

Entry into workforce	**Career peak**	**Retirement**

Entry into workforce	**Career peak**	**Retirement**

Actual time

YOUR FAMILY TIMELINE

Ideal time

Single	**Married with children**	**Other dependents/ elder parent(s)**

Single	**Married with children**	**Other dependents/ elder parent(s)**

Actual time

What about your other priorities?

Most of us have several goals that we set for ourselves simultaneously, and some may be more important than others. In considering whether you will take a risk, you need to look at your other priorities. Ask yourself, "If I pursue this goal at this time, will any of my other life goals be undermined? If so, which is the most important?"

Let's go back to Karen's situation. She had several goals: advancing her career, seeing the world, having a social life, dating, and ultimately settling down. Karen rated their importance to her while considering how they would be affected by her relocating to Brussels.

KAREN'S PRIORITIES

| **Advancing career** | **Seeing the world** | **Dating and social life** |

In Karen's words: "I'm committed to advancing my career. Now is the time to do it. I am also concerned about whether I will find men to date. I do want to meet someone in the next few years and settle down. I know that in a worse case scenario, if I don't find my personal life abroad fulfilling, I can return to the United States after a year."

Valentina Tereshkova (1937–present)
Valentina had no formal pilot training but was an amateur parachutist. She volunteered her service and was accepted into the Soviet cosmonaut program. She's credited as the first woman in space.

──

Now complete this exercise for yourself. It may seem simple, but it will force you to see the effect one action will have on the other aspects of your life. Write down your top three priorities. Which is most important? Label them accordingly. How does this line up with the risk you are considering taking?

YOUR PRIORITIES

_____   _____   _____

Part Three: Gut Sense

A key factor in making a decision to take a risk is paying attention to your gut sense. Here's where you turn your head off and connect with your heart. I believe our inner voice is our best counsel; the problem is that we are doing so much all the time that we don't listen to it. We are always evolving, and when we trust our instincts we make the right decisions.

A colleague of mine, Julie Menin, knew that she wanted to give back to the community when she started her nonprofit organization after September 11, 2001. Though she was already a successful restaurant owner, she started Wall Street Rising, an organization aimed at revitalizing the area of New York City that was hit hardest by the attacks. Julie explains, "I think if it's something you believe strongly in, then it's worth taking the risk. Wall Street Rising has been a labor of love, and the difference we are making has motivated the staff. They are energized by what we do." While the organization was germinated by tragedy, today it has grown to serve over 30,000 residences, businesses, and cultural institutions.

Here is an exercise to help you get in touch with your own wise coach that's there when you turn inward.

Inner Guidance

Take a moment to find a place where you feel comfortable, like a favorite chair in your living room or bedroom. Close your eyes and breathe deeply. Don't be distracted by the thoughts that come to mind. Allow yourself to relax. As you do, ask yourself: Is taking this risk right for me? Then wait for an answer. You will get a sign showing what you should do.

When Karen did this, she felt an excitement well up inside her. At that moment, she knew she would be going to Brussels. Like Karen, some women have heard simple "yes" or "no" answers. I had an opportunity to go on vacation, but work was busier than I had anticipated. I wasn't sure if it was right for me to go abroad on my trip and was wavering back and forth (something I don't want you to do!). I did my plus and minus list and saw that I had the resources to take action and the staff lined up to manage our projects, but I was still indecisive. When I sat quietly I realized it was a Best Bet and booked the tour immediately. Right away I felt a sense of relief that I had made the right choice. Whatever your signal might be, go with it.

Since the beginning of this chapter, you've been looking at your goal to figure out if it's a Best Bet, a No Go, or a Not Now. Well, what is it? If it's a Best Bet, great! You will continue to take action to make your goal a reality. If you found out it's a No Go or Not Now, you'll table it. A Not Now might be that you want a promotion, but given the economic climate and the consolidation of your company, that's not going to happen for quite some time. And at some later point, you will revisit taking action. A No Go could be that you have young children and your partner is locked into a job in the States, so the likelihood of your taking a global assignment is nil.

Keep using the Risk Quotient on other potential goals until you find a Best Bet.

Your Risk-Taker Type

Now that we've tested your risk against the Risk Quotient, it's time to find out what type of risk-taker you are. Think about the questions on the next two pages; the answers you choose will classify your risk-taking style. Keep in mind that this quiz is designed to identify two extreme risk-taking personalities. While you probably possess some qualities of each and likely fall somewhere in the middle, choose the answers that best describe your experience.

Risk-Taker Quiz

1. Your company wants you to relocate from Boston to Paris, France. *Your initial thought is:*
   a. Will I be able to move away from everything I've worked so hard for here?
   b. I wonder what the view of Paris will be from my new office.
2. Your personal motto is closer to:
   a. Slow and steady wins the race.
   b. The fastest way from point A to point B is a straight line.
3. You're redecorating your living room. The perfect couch is over budget. You:
   a. Hold off, consult your finances, and get advice from friends on what you should do.
   b. Take the couch then and there because something that perfect doesn't come along every day.
4. Which term better describes you?
   a. The Anchor—you value security for yourself and your loved ones most.
   b. The Trailblazer—you break barriers and push yourself to new levels of success.

5. How would you describe your surroundings?
   a. Comfortable—you like to be surrounded by what you know.
   b. Ever changing—you like the exotic, crazy, and exciting.
6. On a day-to-day basis, your decision-making style is more:
   a. Detail oriented—you are a perfectionist and details are most important to you.
   b. Big picture oriented—details are overlooked or ignored sometimes.

It's time to add up your scores. If you have more **A** answers, you are what I call a "turtle"—you take a long time to reach each decision, and sometimes your conservative nature hinders your ability to take Smart Risks. If you have more **B** answers, you are a "hare"—it's your nature to take risks, but sometimes you make snap decisions that can hurt you.

As you might have guessed, the "turtle" and the "hare" are two sides of the same coin. Whichever category you fall into, I want you to move toward the other side. If you are a turtle, be bolder: use your heart and gut more in making a decision about taking a risk. If you are a hare, let your head guide the way: analyze the pros and cons before taking the leap.

Changing can be difficult, and you'll need to move beyond your comfort zone. Let the strategies of victorious risk-takers support you to do this.

═══════════ *TRAILBLAZER* ═══════════
Barbara Walters (1931–present)
In October 1976, Barbara became the first female co-anchor on a network evening news program. This journalism pioneer has since solidified her hard-working reputation as host of programs like 20/20, The Barbara Walters Special, and The View.

Four Risk-Taking Strategies

However you approach risk-taking, you can use the following strategies to help move you forward.

Strategy #1: Do the "Head Work," but Trust Your Heart

As we know, successful women analyze the pros and cons of a situation; they look at the timing of an action as well as the other priorities in their lives. But they don't stop there. Ginger Kreutzer, a single mother of two says, "I do follow my intuition. Many of the decisions I make are based on instinct and then the logic comes around to support the decision."

Here are some of the signals that may indicate your desire to move forward:

- You feel an inner excitement about doing something new that you can't shake.

- You try to overcome every objection for not taking the risk.
- You are already lining up your team to make "it" happen.

Let's look at Mindy's story. Mindy is an example of a woman who has made headway in her career using all of her faculties. She moved to Washington, D.C. right after college and took the first job she was offered because she was afraid she wouldn't find something else. Working as a Congressional office assistant was a good entry-level job, but the slow law-making processes frustrated her. In college, she wanted to pursue a career in visual communications. She says, "Somehow I lost track of that. Several of my friends encouraged me to move to New York, the hub of the entertainment industry, and find a job in this field. That felt right and with their support, I took the leap. I looked around this time before I accepted my current job. I learn something new about media every day at my new job, and I'm so busy I have no time to feel bored."

Turtles: Thinking things out is important in deciding whether or not to take a risk. However, if the pluses outweigh the minuses and you're still hesitant to move, listen to your inner counsel that's advising you to GO.

Hares: The pressure to advance may be intense at certain points in your career. Aim to make decisions not just on impulse, but considering the larger picture: your present and future goals.

Strategy #2: You Can't Lose,
Even If You Fail

Even if you fail, it's worth taking the risk because of the invaluable lessons you will learn. If the risk doesn't pan out, you've still moved to another level and you have more experience than you had before. You now have built-in knowledge to guard against making similar mistakes in the future.

Sophia's story is an example of this. She was ready to take a risk, but knew failure was a possibility. She says, "I was respected as an office manager at my company, but it wasn't what I wanted to be doing anymore. Human Resources interested me and I wanted to develop programs for employees. We lacked work/life policies to help employees with childcare and eldercare. On my own time, I researched what other companies were doing and with some coaching from a friend, I positioned a business case for the initiative. I was anxious about presenting these ideas to my boss, but I scheduled a meeting anyway. I knew that I had done my homework and was prepared to quit sometime in the future if things didn't work out. Well, they didn't. He thanked me for the 'good work,' but said they weren't about to make that investment now. This was something employees had to do for themselves. Of course, I was upset. But I really have no regrets because I weighed in on creating change. The experience propelled me to look for another job, and I ultimately took my expertise somewhere else." For Sophia, it was better to risk and not get what she wanted than to play it safe. She said it was like skiing; if you learn to ski and never fall, you aren't making much progress.

Turtles: *Sometimes you spend too much time safeguarding yourself in case you might fail. Remember, even failure has its benefits. As Annette Martinez, Assistant Vice President at State Farm notes, "If you fail and learn how to recover and grow from it, then you'll never be seen as a failure. You have to take calculated risks every day and some of them are not going to work, and that's okay. Just learn, recover, and move forward—and you'll teach others to do that too."*

Hares: *You are often passionate about the risks you undertake. Just make sure that you take a thorough approach as you move forward; use logic.*

Strategy #3: Don't Do It Alone: Start Mobilizing the Troops!

At every step of your risk-taking process, get advice from people who can support your new venture. It is never too early to mobilize your team. Let them know your passions as well as your concerns. Get them excited about the possibilities of your vision, but elicit honest feedback from them, too. You may need to make adjustments to your plan based on their recommendations. More about this in Step Three.

In Mindy's case, the knowledge that she had an existing group of friends to fall back on eased her career move. For both Karen and Sophia as well, advice from others about their situations helped them move forward. The bottom line? Don't do it alone!

Turtles: Sometimes you analyze too much without reaching out to others.

Hares: In trying to get to the final results as fast as possible, you often choose to get there alone.

Turtles and Hares: Ask for help!

Here's an example of a woman whose Smart Risk was to build a network of support at her company. When DuPont Marketing Director Brenda Thomas began at her company, there were few people of color there, and only 1 or 2 percent of them were women. She says, "I wanted to engage people in a dialogue about racism, but I didn't want to create a backlash. I wanted people to begin thinking about what was going on. I felt that people would want to talk if they felt comfortable—if the conversations happened informally. I took my time and the conversations began. Together as black women, we talked about our invisibility. We developed forums to bring others out and formed a network. Later, we became aware that we needed to embrace white women and other issues. To do that we knew everyone would have to deal with a whole lot of misperception, anger, and guilt. So we did that. We came to understand the core gender issues that were affecting all of us. We all wanted to feel we could succeed in the corporation."

Strategy #4: If It Looks Like a GO, Take Action

Winners don't hesitate. They analyze and then act. Think of Karen: after making her list and weighing the pros and cons, she accepted the job in Brussels. Recall Mindy: after deciding that her Congressional job wasn't right for her, she moved to New York City and pursued her career vision, never looking back. Remember Sophia's resolve to go forward and present her proposal, even though it was risky.

If you wait too long with your Best Bet, the opportunity might pass.

Turtles: If things line up, don't procrastinate—Just do it!

Hares: Acting immediately is not a problem for you. But you must act when the risk is a Best Bet. Use the Risk Quotient.

More than likely you will achieve your goal, but you may not. Even the best-laid plans can take wrong turns due to unforeseen circumstances. Instead of getting frustrated when disasters happen, plan ahead! Always have a variety of "if that should happen" contingency plans to help you navigate through worst-case scenarios. They can be very simple: going back to your old job if offered the chance, using the experience you've gained to land another job, or forming a partnership so that you share the responsibilities in achieving your goal. You may find that, in creating an "if that should happen" plan, you consider a strategic option that you hadn't thought of before.

Not Nows and No Gos

If you've found that your goal has worked out to be a Not Now or a No Go, don't get discouraged. It takes courage to acknowledge that something isn't right. If your goal is a Not Now, is there anything you can do to revise it so that it's more viable for right now? If not, simply go back to Step One and select a new goal. The same goes for a No Go. Just because that goal wasn't worth pursuing doesn't mean the next one won't be. Move on. Now is the time for you to take a risk. You just need to select the right one!

Quick Tips

- Smart Risk-Taking will help you go to the next level. As you take action, you are inviting something new to come in. Most likely, it will be something better.

- Use the Risk Quotient: Analyze the pros and cons; consider timing and your other priorities; trust your gut sense.
- Be conscious of your risk-taking type: Make adjustments by following the examples of victorious risk-takers.

POWER LINK: For additional success strategies of risk-takers, go to www.womenworking.com/success/

STEP THREE

TEAM WITH WINNERS

DECLARATION:

I reach out for support with enthusiasm.
People are attracted to my commitment and passion
and help me achieve my goal.

QUALITIES OF A SMART RISK-TAKER:

Passionate
Enthusiastic
Team player

I think the most fabulous thing . . . can be when you develop . . .
relationships over time, and you really do begin to build
a constituency. The people who have worked for you,
the people who have worked with you, as well as
the people you've worked for, can become a very powerful
set of voices that support you.

—Anne Mulcahy,
Chairman and CEO, Xerox

Our power as businesswomen lies in our ability to form strong alliances with other professionals, to elicit their help, and to be ready to offer ours when asked. And we need to reach out to both men and women in order to build these networks that will aid in our risk-taking process.

Phoebe Eng, Creative Director of The Opportunity Agenda, feels strongly that mentors are essential to move us forward. She says, "Advancement doesn't happen primarily through pulling oneself up by the bootstraps. I always cringe when I hear people say that they did it all by themselves and that it just took hard work and trust in the fact that things will happen for them. To a certain point that may be true, but it isn't the key ingredient to getting ahead at work. Opportunities happen when someone in charge believes in you and takes a chance on your behalf by opening a door."

The same is true when you have targeted your Smart Risk. Yes, you will make it happen—but not alone. You will need the help of others to get over the hurdles and benchmark your actions. That was also the experience for two out of three women who responded to our Risk-Taking Survey. They reported needing the support of others before making a big move.

This chapter focuses on how to create your risk-taking network: a few people who will help you keep the momentum going and give you invaluable feedback.

How Do You Choose These Supporters?

Before identifying your risk as a Best Bet in Step Two, you probably reached out for advice from a colleague to confirm your decision. This person may be someone you'll want to include on your team. You are looking for two to three people with skill sets that complement yours.

When choosing these supporters, ask yourself: What expertise will I need to follow-through on my goal? What do I bring to the table, and what can others offer? For example, if your Best Bet is to start a newsletter at your company, (giving you increased visibility because you will be featured as a columnist), who can create a budget with you and help sell your proposal to management? Or if you want to transition into a new business, for example, which people have industry expertise and can offer sales and marketing advice?

In order to create these allies, you must be the one to take the initiative, but you may not be accustomed to asking for help.

Why Don't We Reach Out More?

Relationships take time to build. And time is at a premium for women like us. Between regular work assignments and family responsibilities, we are overscheduled as it is. Also, as women, we often have to work twice as hard as our male counterparts to advance. We may fear that asking for help would make us appear vulnerable, which would diminish the capable image we've been projecting at work.

You can reach out from a position of strength by carefully selecting those people who have the expertise you need and asking them for specific feedback. This is quite different from appearing vague or confused, which will turn them off. Establishing alliances with colleagues both inside and outside of your company will be the key to achieving your goal.

===== *TRAILBLAZER* =====

Ann Bancroft (1955–present)

Ann joined an all-male team to become the first woman to reach the North Pole by sled and on foot in 1986. Later, she led the first women's team to reach the South Pole on skis.

Powerful women know that asking for help is invaluable. As Louise Francesconi, President of Missile Systems at Raytheon, revealed, "I've always been willing to expose myself to what I need to know better. I could never have moved through Raytheon giving the impression that I know everything. The risk was allowing people to see that I needed help. Do I ever regret that? No."

When putting together your risk-taking team, it's important to reach out to people of diverse backgrounds. If you do, you'll have a broader understanding of the challenges and opportunities before you. This is true in general about creating meaningful alliances at work. Patti Bellinger, Group Vice President Executive Development, Diversity & Inclusion at BP, advises, "You need to build relationships with people who are different. You have to give them permission to tell you what you don't know, which is how you learn. You have to make it safe for people to talk openly and honestly to you, to provide candid feedback. It's also very important to be generous, and to assume the best of people."

Honest feedback is essential in your risk-taking process. Do your supervisors and colleagues give it? Probably not. Are you in the habit of asking for it? Probably not again. Why do you think this is? I'd venture to say that it's because we may take things too personally. By doing so, we miss out on valuable information that could help us advance.

One woman told me that she thought her boss couldn't be direct with her because he was afraid she'd break down and cry. She knew she'd have to get him talking or else she'd be stuck in the same job for years. We will also need our risk-taking team to be candid with us from the very beginning. Let them know that you are choosing them because of their expertise and their ability to be frank and direct with you. By doing this you are opening the lines of communication. Their feedback may be something you don't want to hear at times, but probably something you need to know.

=== *TRAILBLAZER* ===

Frances Perkins (1882–1965)

Frances became the first woman Cabinet member after being appointed by Franklin Delano Roosevelt in 1933. As U.S. Secretary of Labor she promoted the adoption of a number of innovative programs, helping to draft the Social Security Act.

I mobilized my own risk-taking network to help jump-start my company, Creative Expansions, Inc., by reaching out to pros in the entertainment field. One was a senior producer of a prestigious production company. The questions I directed to him were mostly about timing—determining when I should launch the company given the climate of the industry. I had wanted to start the business a year before he thought I should. I hadn't expected this feedback and, as you can imagine, I was somewhat disappointed. But I trusted his expertise and delayed the start of my venture. He has been very helpful through the years, and I've been able to support him too, hiring him for some of my company's subsequent productions.

A friend of mine who is a high-powered media executive was my confidante. I went to her for feedback on dealing with difficult people during the start-up of the company. I remember telling her about one incident that was frustrating and downright demoralizing. Her response was to look me straight in the eye and say: "Next!" Her message was loud and clear: don't waste your energy with "small stuff"—move on to what's most important. This helped me to stay focused on what was important as I advanced.

Selecting Your Risk-Taking Mentors

What expertise do you need from other people to accomplish your goal? Who are the people that possess these skills and will give you honest feedback? Think of women and men you've known at your current job, past assignments, community and professional associations. What does each one have to offer? How do they complement your skills?

You are about to create a prospect list in order to assemble at least two risk-taking allies. Have four people or more on your list. You need to have backups in case your first two choices are unavailable. Even if you think someone won't have time, or doesn't know you well enough, put the name down on your list. You'd be surprised who may respond if you approach them in the right way.

As an example, if your goal is to open a gourmet food store in your hometown, and in Step Two you assessed that it is a Smart Risk, you want to know what expertise is necessary to carry this out. If your background is in marketing and you've worked in a different industry, someone on your team needs to have dealt with food distributors and salespeople. In addition, you may want your second person to be an entrepreneur whose recent start-up business has been successful.

Now, it's time for you to review your prospects by filling in the information below. Rank them according to how helpful they can be to achieving your goal. You will also be asked to clarify your own skills, among other things.

My venture: _____

_____

_____

_____

_____

_____

What I bring to the table (my strengths): _____

_____

_____

_____

_____

_____

What I need from other people (skills that complement mine): _____

_____

_____

_____

_____

_____

PROSPECTS FOR MY RISK-TAKING TEAM

Names	Skills
1. _____	1. _____
2. _____	2. _____
3. _____	3. _____
4. _____	4. _____

Let's focus on the top two people on your list. Think about how you will approach them to elicit their support. Plan this carefully—it's important that you come from your power center when you do. If you need to, brainstorm best-case scenarios with a friend or colleague. For example, you may know that your prospect comes in early and has coffee in the company cafeteria—that might be a good time to speak with her. Also, do your homework. Get to know as much as you can about her: what projects she is working on, information about her family, etc.

Approaching Your Prospects

When contacting a prospect, follow these four simple steps:

Introduce yourself. Tell her who you are and try to establish a common bond—bring up a similar interest that you might have, talk to her about her family or an organization she is involved with. It is very important that you don't start by asking her to be part of your team. That will turn her off.

Acknowledge her. Don't hold back from praising one of her accomplishments—most people like to be appreciated for their hard work. If possible, highlight something she's done recently. Give her the message that you've done your homework and are eager to align with her.

Convey what you are doing. Be passionate about your goal. She will more than likely be attracted to your mission if you share your enthusiasm with her. First impressions count, so maintain eye contact. You want to appear confident.

Ask for what you need. Make sure to pose your question in a succinct way. Don't put her on the spot. Say you'll follow-up later this week by calling her office to see if she's available to support your venture.

Important: When you follow-up, be prepared for the answer to go either way. Always be gracious—people are busy, and if they turn you down now, it doesn't mean they won't be available in the future.

━━━━━ *TRAILBLAZER* ━━━━━

Elizabeth Boit (1849–1932)

In 1888 Elizabeth became the first woman to establish ownership in the textile industry as part-owner of Winship, Boit & Company. An innovative company leader, she offered workers benefits not common at the time, including a profit-sharing plan open to all employees.

Here's how Diana approached one of her prospects at a networking event for female executives. She attended hoping to meet a woman who could give her feedback on the career move she was about to make, which she had identified as a Smart Risk. There was a panel of high-level industry leaders at the session and a cocktail reception afterwards. Diana had been working as a broker in the New York office of a large financial company. During a downturn in the economy, she was offered a position as the Human Resources director for the Dallas office. She would be responsible for staffing, downsizing if necessary, and personnel matters. By taking this position, she would go off a commission structure, but would make about $10,000 more than her current annual base salary. She considered this offer a Best Bet: sufficient money, management title, and relocating to her hometown of Dallas. Everything lined up for her to take the job, yet the uncertainty of such a big change made her nervous. Although her former boss had advised her to do it, she wanted to touch base with an economist whose job was to analyze industry trends.

Diana's Four Step Approach:

1. **Introduce.** After the panelists spoke, hoards of people surrounded them to ask questions. Diana waited patiently. She approached the female economist and told her how much she appreciated her comments. Diana asked for her business card and said she would like to

call her to touch base. She was not specific about what she wanted to talk about; it wasn't the right time to do that.

Setting up the appointment. She followed up the next day by calling to set a time to meet. Diana's voice was confident. It was easy to get through to the woman because she had a business card with a direct number. She told the economist's assistant that her boss had agreed to a 20-minute meeting within the next two weeks. "Best in person, but phone would work too if that is the only way," Diana suggested. (Although face-to-face meetings are preferable, they are not always possible.) A conference call was set for 10 a.m. on Tuesday of the following week.

2. **Acknowledge.** During the conference call, she thanked the economist for the insights she had shared on the panel and made sure to bring up one point that the economist seemed passionate about.

   Do your homework. Doing research beforehand will not only prepare you for that important conversation, but it may present you with information you hadn't anticipated. Diana found that the economist moved back home after a three-year assignment in another city. Since the economist had gone through an experience similar to hers, Diana decided she'd ask her for advice about negotiating a good relocation package.

3. and 4. Convey and Ask

Be Specific. Diana briefly talked about her offer and said she would probably take it. The economist thought that the market would be lack-luster in the next year and confirmed that it might be a good move. She also gave her a few tips about negotiating a relocation package. Diana was appreciative and asked if she could call periodically, promising to keep in touch.

Why was Diana's encounter successful? She picked the right person, stayed focused during the conversation, and kept her questions short and to the point.

TRAILBLAZER

Diane Crump (1949–present)

Diane Crump became the first female jockey to ride in the Kentucky Derby in 1970, the horseracing event's ninety-sixth year.

Mutually Beneficial Relationships

Being gracious goes a long way. Diana will keep in touch with her risk-taking mentor, but it won't only be to report her progress. She will look for ways to give back: perhaps sending her an article of interest or relaying some information she will learn in the trenches.

Building mutually beneficial relationships is key to successful risk-taking. No matter how senior the people that you're reaching out to are, you have something to offer them. This point was clearly demonstrated at a panel I moderated for a Fortune 500 company. The company president was introduced by a young woman who had mentored him—it's called "mentoring up." Although she was his junior in terms of rank, she worked in the field and could fill him in on how employees felt at different levels of the organization.

You'll be selecting your network as you follow up with your prospects in the not-too-distant future. When you've confirmed your team, fill out the information below. This will help you to clarify what you need from each one and get right to the point when you connect with them.

MY RISK-TAKING NETWORK

Name of Person: _____

Role(s):   Coach and confidante

I will: Ask them for advice before taking difficult actions
Report my wins, report my losses
Share frustrations that arise

Name of Person: _____

Role(s):   Industry expert

I will: Ask them for info about the climate of the industry
Keep abreast of technological advances

═══════════════ *TRAILBLAZER* ═══════════════

Oprah Winfrey (1954–present)

Oprah's talk show debuted in the 1980s and remains at the top of the ratings. Oprah has expanded her enterprises to include several major studio movies, a lifestyle magazine, her own production company, and service-based advocacy programs.

Get the Competitive Edge

In order for you to achieve your goal, you will need to commit yourself 100 percent—that means you must be willing to do whatever it takes to achieve your goal. And one of the things you'll need to do is to sharpen your risk-taking skills. Our Risk-Taking Survey cited focus and communication as two of the *most* important attributes for success.

Stay Focused

It's so easy to get off track and lose sight of your goal. Self-doubt would rear its ugly head when I was about to take a major risk. An early coach of mine, Roz Relin, taught me to concentrate on what was important. She would say, "Helene, keep your eye on the doughnut, not the hole."

Pfizer's Senior VP of Global Research and Development and Director of its biggest laboratory, Nancy Hutson, confronted the doubts that kept creeping in when she was about to take the biggest risk of her career. She didn't get sidetracked and was able to lead what is now a 5,000-person, highly evolved organization. She says, "What I did was start a new group, the strategic management organization for Pfizer. The R&D function of the company needed a strategic planning management function. I was a Ph.D. biochemist/physiologist and knew nothing about strategic planning management. But I felt that there was a real opportunity to make a broad contribution. I was willing to go and try to figure out what it would take to do it. By taking a risk where I didn't know a whole lot, where I could only lead by influence, I was able to show management that I had a lot of skill and talent—that I could function at a very high level in the organization, not just in the job I was doing."

My friend Estelle, a senior manager, shared with me a technique that helps her stay on track with whatever is in front of her. She says, "I think of myself at the center of a wheel. The spokes emanating from me represent my work, family, social, and community responsibilities. I play many roles in my life, and I've learned to focus my energies on one area at a time. For example, I head the local PTA. That part of me isn't in the foreground during my workday. Nor is the fact that I'm a mother uppermost on my mind when I'm dealing with how to strategize a new product launch. And I do this with peace of mind, because I've sought a lot of help along the way so that I know my children are well taken care of when I'm not around. I rely on my baby-sitter (my mom) and my husband, who helps out with some of the children's emergencies."

Celeste Clark, Senior VP of Corporate Affairs at Kellogg's, believes it's all about priorities. She advises, "Focus on the big things you need to concentrate on to make a difference versus those that are nice but not necessary. Know what you need to accomplish within a certain time period and meet that requirement. Then work to establish trust and credibility with the people you're working with to make things happen."

Communicate Powerfully

You must be able to present your risk-taking goal and action steps in a way that will inspire others to become part of your team. The words and style you use are extremely important. It's not only essential to speak positively, but also to acknowledge another person's style and communicate in a way that will motivate them.

I find it useful to talk their language, not my own. In other words, observe how they communicate and follow their lead. For example, if a person frames things in bottom-line terms, converse with them in that way. If they are storytellers, use your dramatic flair and tell stories to them too.

This communication strategy became obvious to me after a frustrating experience with a boss several years ago. When I was working at a newspaper in the 1980s, I had a supervisor whose expertise was marketing. He communicated in short, focused sentences. My style was very different from his. I felt more comfortable telling stories, but when I did I noticed he became impatient. After a while, I started to talk his language. I'd come into his office and present the increase or decrease of product sales in percentages. My statements were short and to the point. Guess what happened? Our communication became much better.

When he was promoted, I offered my new boss information in this same way, but he seemed uninterested in what I was saying. When I observed him more closely, I realized that he was a storyteller. He didn't want to get down to business right away. So I switched my way of relating to him and, of course, everyone was happier as a result.

Another element to powerful communication is right timing. The other person needs to be receptive and ready to hear what you have to say. For example, if you know that your immediate supervisor is responsible for downsizing your division in the next month, then now is not the time to ask him to support a new venture that may be risky. You would want to wait for a more opportune time.

No one ever stops learning, so don't get complacent. Keep honing your skills. Not only will you become a better risk-taker, but a more attractive and knowledgeable human being.

Quick Tips

- Recognize the importance of a risk-taking network and start getting yours together.

- Create a prospect list of about four names. Be specific: What type of expertise do you need from each person? Use the four-step approach for contacting a potential prospect (Introduce, Acknowledge, Convey, Ask).
- When your team is confirmed, write down their roles (i.e., coach, confidante, industry expert) and what you expect from them. It may be appropriate for you to explain your expectations to each individual so that all of you are aligned. This will help you make the most of everyone's time.
- Stay focused and communicate powerfully!

POWER LINK: Go to www.womenworking.com/books/ to find books that offer insights to sharpen your risk-taking skills.

Step Four

Take a Leap and Come from Strength

Declaration:

I take action toward achieving my goal knowing that whatever the result, it will be beneficial to me. There is no such thing as failure because I view all situations as opportunities to learn something new about myself.

Qualities of a Smart Risk-Taker:

Courage
Strength
Wisdom

Never be too afraid to make a change when you know
it is the right thing to do. In being safe,
one misses out on huge potential upside benefits.

—Ellen Griffith,
Manager, Accenture

Follow-Through

We are strong, resilient, and have great stamina. Sometimes when we feel "stretched," we may not think that we have all the resources to accomplish what we need to, but we do! Once you have identified a Smart Risk, the process of making it happen may seem daunting. And that may inhibit you from getting started. Impeding obstacles can cause you to doubt your ability to achieve a goal. At these times, it's essential to connect with your inner strength—taking action, moving forward on faith. Here's an example of when I was able to follow through during a trying time in my life.

I was doubtful of my ability to withstand the stress of my mother's illness a few years ago. Her getting sick took my family by surprise. I had just finished a television program on quality of life issues for cancer patients, thanked my staff for a job well done, and went home. I came in the door, said hello to my then 12-year-old son, and was about to relax when the phone rang. It was my mother calling from the emergency room of a local hospital. She had taken herself there because she was jaundiced. Since I was the daughter who lived closest to her, I went over right away.

That was the beginning of one of the most traumatic periods in my life. In the next week, my mother was diagnosed with pancreatic cancer. She underwent surgery and lived for another four months.

Stretched was not the word for how I felt. I had a new television show coming up to prepare for, had to get my son, Heath, ready for school, and wanted to comfort my mom during her last days. I found a way to do it all by compartmentalizing my tasks. I made sure Heath had what he needed before he went out the door. From 9 a.m. to 6 p.m. I worked on my projects, and in the evening I visited my mother in the hospital (sometimes crying on my cell phone to a friend before walking into her room). With the support I received from coworkers, I was able to prioritize what was most important to do. During that time, I led a panel of top executives for a widely publicized event. In retrospect, I can't believe I did it all, but I did.

TRAILBLAZER

Maya Lin (1959–present)

Following a national competition, Maya was chosen to design the Vietnam Veterans Memorial in Washington, D.C. An American architect and sculptor, she submitted the winning design while still a senior at Yale University.

Women who are Smart Risk-Takers exhibit great courage. They aren't satisfied with the status quo, and they possess the strength to overcome obstacles in their paths. And you have that ability, too. Just think back to a crisis in your life. Think of what happened and how, initially, you didn't think you would be able to meet the challenge. But you did. What resources in yourself did you reach for? Who assisted you with advice or was willing to simply listen to what you were going through? Who pitched in to help when you needed her to? For me, the love I felt for my mother was stronger than any fear or fatigue I was experiencing. I knew I'd show up each day and I did—for my mom, for Heath, for my company, and for myself.

We have great resources within us, as well as the resiliency to spring back no matter what consequences result from the actions we take. So why not take a Smart Risk? Even if you fail, you can handle it—and learn from it.

To be a successful risk-taker, you admit to past mistakes and use them as stepping-stones to new successes. Michelle Gloeckler of The Hershey Company has a positive spin on this. She says, "I admit my mistakes. Out loud. In front of a lot of people. It's therapeutic! When I do something wrong, I will admit it, correct it, and state that it won't happen again as quickly as I can." That's the attitude!

In order for any athlete to get better at her sport, she takes in stride the strengths and weaknesses of her game. Each time a soccer team runs off the field, win or lose, the coach starts thinking about what they can do better the next time they play. Were they aggressive enough, did they shoot for the goal? Pass to players? Was the other team's defense stronger than theirs?

This fictitious soccer team demonstrates the stamina it takes to follow through and achieve your Smart Risk. Now you are almost ready to execute your Best Bet. You must stay focused and not get sidetracked. Don't let self-doubt creep in. If anything, learn from past mistakes.

Think about the last time you were about to take a risk. Did you let your fear get in the way? Did you weaken your ability to achieve your goal with questions, nit-picking every detail? Did you put off taking a risk because you felt too "stretched" in other areas of your life? If so, you don't want to do that again. This chapter will give you ammunition to remain on target and take your Smart Risk. But in order to do so, you'll need to reflect on habits that keep you stuck and afraid to move, such as procrastination, second-guessing, and perfectionism.

Take the following Personality Type Quiz to identify the traits that can slow you down and distract you from fulfilling your goal. For each question, the options may seem contrived, but choose the one you resonate with the most.

Personality Type Quiz

Your boss assigns you as manager of a team project. You:
a. Take charge by creating a plan of action without consulting your team for input. As usual, you end up doing some of the tasks you've assigned to others yourself!

b. Know that on one level you are qualified to be in charge, but on another level you doubt your abilities.

c. Think, "I'll start my game plan next week."

d. Think, "Okay. Let me call the team together, get their feedback, and get started."

It comes time to delegate responsibility for the project. You end up:

a. Constantly checking up on everyone and then redoing most of the work they've done, convinced that you are the only one who can do it right.

b. Being indecisive about whom to assign work to.

c. Giving out work to those on your team that e-mail or call you, and waiting for the others to contact you before considering them.

d. Doing your job and letting your teammates do theirs. You trust the people you have brought together.

You would describe your office as:

a. In order. You organized your office into a special system that works for you and probably doesn't make sense to anyone else.

b. Cluttered. You make two copies of everything you send out or receive, plus the drafts in case you make a mistake and have to justify it.

c. Stale. All around your office are projects that are long overdue. You still need to finish them but haven't found the time to do so.

d. Neat. It is somewhat organized so that you can work efficiently.

It's 5:30 on Friday. Your workday typically ends at 6:00 but you have piles of papers sitting on your desk. You:

a. Stay all evening until everything is finished.

b. Feel stressed about all you have to do but leave at 6:00, taking your stress with you.

c. Leave without giving the work a second thought—you did all that you could. You're used to letting things pile up.

d. Maybe stay an extra hour, knowing you'll tackle the rest on Monday.

In general you feel _____ at work.

a. Overbooked

b. Anxious

c. Distracted

d. Confident

You have written a proposal that you will present to the CEO in five minutes. You:

a. Are exhausted! You were up all night perfecting the presentation.

b. Have your assistant reread it for the hundredth time because you're worried you didn't make it strong enough.

c. Are still finishing the last section.

d. Breathe deeply and give yourself a pep talk: "I've been planning and working on this for weeks. I'll do great!"

Your boss is leaving the company. She informs you that the company is looking to fill the spot and encourages you to go for the job. You:

a. Compile your résumé, write out a list of all your accomplishments, and debate whether or not you are really qualified to follow in her footsteps.

b. Consider it briefly before determining that you know there is no way they would really consider you, so you don't take action.

c. Tell her, "Thanks" and that you'll follow up with her next week. And you know you may never do that.

d. Set up a meeting with the vice president of human resources to explore the possibility of this promotion.

Now it's time to tabulate. Look at your answers and see which personality type matches you best:

Type A (mostly As)—The Perfectionist

Type B (mostly Bs)—The Second-Guesser

Type C (mostly Cs)—The Procrastinator

Type D (mostly Ds)—The Moderate

If You're the Perfectionist . . .

You are not at all shocked by the outcome of this quiz. Your whole life you have known that you are indeed a perfectionist in every sense of the word. You work relentlessly, perfecting small, insignificant details because everything must be done flawlessly. You are hardly ever satisfied, refusing to recognize your achievements or the achievements of others and instead looking to what else still needs to be done. When you delegate responsibility, you end up micromanaging and frustrating those around you. The outcomes of your projects are exceptional and you are dedicated to excellence, but is it worth the cost of agonizing over every detail? You tend to anticipate the worst-case scenarios, and work yourself up by projecting problems instead of thinking about positive outcomes.

Strategies for Overcoming Perfectionism

- You are not being fair to yourself or others. Use positive mind-talk and tell yourself, "Everything will get done, even if it's not done perfectly."
- When you finish one task, take a quick break before beginning another, and acknowledge what you've accomplished. You will feel more fulfilled by doing this.
- Stop underestimating yourself. Go for that job promotion or take the next step toward doing something out of the ordinary. You are more capable than you think you are, and you'll discover that as soon as you let go of petty details.

If You're the Second-Guesser . . .

A Second-Guesser is someone who decides to make a move, has done all her homework, but then gets cold feet. As she takes a step forward, she may take two steps backward. If you've done this before, you know that this type of behavior can drive you crazy.

Strategies for Overcoming Second-Guessing

- Don't look back. If you get cold feet, reaffirm your goal as a Best Bet and move on.
- Understand that life is full of choices. They can be as complex as moving across the country, or as simple as taking a different route to work one morning. If we spent time debating these decisions individually, we'd never move at all. Put yourself in the hands of fate, knowing that you have the ability to learn a brilliant lesson, no matter what the result.

If You're the Procrastinator . . .

It's hard for you to get motivated. You may even feel intimidated or overwhelmed by a project, so you put things off to a later time, but at what price? If you wait until the last minute to follow through on deadlines, you're forced to maintain an unhealthy crash-and-burn working style.

Strategies for Overcoming Procrastination

- Make a beginning. Take a small step toward your goal and acknowledge what you have done so far. This may seem insignificant given your standards, but it isn't. It will give you momentum to do more.
- Create a checklist for yourself—a timetable of focused actions to take you toward your goal. Do not go past the due dates. If you need to, elicit the support of a coworker to keep you on track.
- Reward yourself, even in a small way, each time you take on an action and accomplish it.

If You're the Moderate . . .

You get things done and accept that you can't avoid making some mistakes. But you learn from them. You are proud of your successes. Keep up that positive attitude. You're a born leader.

When you see people pushing themselves too hard, help them keep a balanced perspective.

Even *you* can have a lapse in judgment or react differently than you normally would. If you find that perfectionism, self-doubt, or procrastination creep in, read over the strategies that we've just mentioned.

Exercise

Examine your past. Write down a risk that you would have liked to have taken, but didn't, and answer the following questions.

Risk: _____

_____

_____

Did procrastination, second-guessing, or perfectionism impede you from taking action? _____

_____

_____

Did something else get in the way? _____

_____

_____

What support would you have needed to do things differently?

_____

_____

_____

We've examined patterns of behavior that can deter us from following through on a Best Bet. Now let's shed light on the subtle thoughts and attitudes that undermine our confidence and our risk-taking ability.

De-Clutter Your Mind

In order to free up your energy to take that Smart Risk, you'll need to become aware of what I call "mind clutter" and accordingly take action. Begin as if you were to sort out and throw away the stuff that's been piling up around your house—only in this case, it's your negative mind-talk that you'll be "talking back to." When you become aware of these destructive thoughts, simply focus your attention on something more productive.

The Mind Clutter Inventory

Be honest with yourself as you fill out the questions below. Reflect on your answers before you write them down.

What do you tell yourself about your abilities that makes you feel worse, not better? _____

_____

_____

Are you generally unforgiving toward people who disappoint you, either on the job or in your personal life? Describe a recent incident when you were disappointed (who was involved, what happened, how you felt about what transpired). _____

_____

_____

Do you feel victimized, passed over for work assignments by supervisors? If so, explain the last time you felt that way. ___

_____

_____

Do you rehash petty grievances? If the answer is "Yes," explain the last time you did this. _____

_____

_____

Do you exaggerate your importance to people? If you do, describe a recent incident when that happened. _____

_____

_____

Do you tell subtle lies, catch yourself, and continue anyway? If the answer is "Yes," explain why you think you do this. ___

_____

_____

Do you often feel superior or inferior to others—not on the same level? If so, describe an instance when you felt this way. Be specific: what was happening at the time? _____

_____

_____

Do you compare yourself to others and discount your accomplishments as a result? If so, when was the last time you did this? _____

_____

_____

If you can relate to any of the above scenarios, you may be limiting yourself in a way that you weren't aware of. I want to support you to change that. The object here is to set aside limiting beliefs that keep you stuck so you can advance.

Let's take a look at strategies to help get you back on track when mind clutter becomes apparent.

EXAMINING MIND CLUTTER

Attitudes that make me feel worse	Overcoming strategy
Blame and lack of forgiveness.	Understand what motivates the people you have a problem with, and practice forgiveness.
Feeling like a victim.	Take responsibility for your part in what has transpired.
Holding onto petty grievances.	Use your energy positively. Focus on the task at hand.

Attitudes that make me feel worse	Overcoming strategy
Exaggerating your importance.	Acknowledge your strengths and weaknesses. It's a great equalizer— you'll realize we all have them.
Telling subtle lies.	Awareness of when you are dishonest is the first step toward becoming more honest.

Clearing mind clutter leaves you open and ready to take on the challenges ahead. Let it go, let it all go. Where you are going is up to you, and the future is looking good. There is no more stalling, no more second-guessing, no more excuses. The time to leap is now. Your adrenaline is pumping. Your blood is flowing. Your mind is clear. You are on the verge of making a move in the right direction. You are ready to take that Smart Risk—so leap!

TRAILBLAZER

Rochelle Jones (1958–present)

In 1994, Rochelle became the first female lieutenant in the New York Fire Department. Later she became a captain and Commanding Officer in Manhattan's Financial District, where she served during the events of September 11, 2001. Now, as Battalion Chief, she is the highest-ranking female in FDNY history.

Quick Tips

- Realize that you have a great deal of inner strength. If you take a Smart Risk that doesn't pan out, your resilience will keep you moving forward.
- Identify habits that slow you down and hinder your ability to follow through: perfectionism, second-guessing, and procrastination.
- Spot these shortcomings when they come up. Knowing that they may have stopped you in the past is motivation to do things differently.
- De-clutter your mind by becoming aware of thoughts and attitudes that hold you back and stop "fueling" them.

POWER LINK: At www.womenworking.com/join/join_nework. php you can join our Member Network to receive a monthly newsletter and keep connected with other Smart Risk-Takers.

Step Five

Claim Victory—
You've Earned It

Declaration:
I acknowledge my accomplishments and experience
my growth. I am grateful for all who have helped
me to succeed. I share my success with
those around me.

Qualities of a Smart Risk-Taker:
Gratitude
Inner reflection
Humility

*There was no history of a woman leading in construction,
and that automatically made it a little more difficult. I didn't
back down, not even during the hard times, and that's what
made me a pioneer. If you really believe in something,
you stay focused, have confidence, stay loyal to what you
believe in, and eventually you will succeed.*

—Barbara Kavovit,
Founder of barbara k!

Congratulations! You've taken a Smart Risk. Despite your fear, you moved forward and took a leap.

Regardless of the results, think about all you've done. You have

- Acknowledged your desire to take a risk and change your life.
- Set a goal.
- Analyzed your Risk Quotient and figured out whether your risk was a Best Bet, a Not Now, or a No Go.
- Identified and formed valuable alliances to achieve your goal.
- Become more aware of how procrastination, second-guessing, or perfectionism can deter your progress.

Regardless of the outcome of the Smart Risk you've taken, you must acknowledge the courage you've demonstrated by taking action. It's not unusual to feel a mixture of emotions at the end of the process, as JoAnn Tennyson experienced. She had been working as an educator for 25 years but wanted something more. After meeting with a career counselor and researching other opportunities, she decided to go back to school to get her Master's degree and become a career counselor herself. She says, "Feelings of exhilaration and a knot in my stomach are my constant companions. I love this time in my life! I feel as much excitement and joy now as I did when I first entered the classroom 30 years ago. We are never too old to risk and find ways to use our gifts to serve others."

Whether You Have Achieved Your Goal or Not—You Are a Winner!

You have not stood still—you've acted on what you thought was a Best Bet and can use all you've learned for future initiatives. Even if your risk did not pan out or the results were different than you expected, this still holds true. Remember, it's better to have taken a leap than not.

TRAILBLAZER

Patsy Takemoto Mink (1927–2002)

Following her graduation from the University of Chicago Law School, Patsy became the first Japanese-American woman to practice law in Hawaii. In 1964, she became the first Asian-American woman elected to Congress where, as a U.S. representative, she championed equal opportunity programs for women.

If you have not achieved what you set out to, you probably know what aspects of your plan may need reworking, and shortly you'll be taking a closer look. Or it may be better to start over, identify a new goal, and use the Risk Quotient to determine if it's a Best Bet. Whatever the case, you have your work cut out for you.

Evaluate Your Risk-Taking Process

Let's take a closer look at each step you've taken along the way. What worked, what didn't? What insights do you have as to why it went well, or didn't, at certain points? What would you have done differently? Review any notes or charts you may have kept, and take a moment to write down your thoughts in the Risk Evaluation Table.

RISK EVALUATION TABLE

Step	Insights	What would you do differently next time?
Step 1: Setting a Goal		
Step 2: The Risk Quotient		

(Continued)

(*Continued*)

Step	Insights	What would you do differently next time?
Step 3: Mobilizing Support		
Step 4: Taking the Leap		

Restate Your Best Bet

You have now joined an elite group of Smart Risk-Takers, and it's important to tell others what you've accomplished. I know it may be uncomfortable for you to do that. It can feel like boasting. Perhaps when you were a young girl, you were taught to be humble and modest. But to keep your achievements to yourself doesn't serve you very well. Bragging is a muscle that lies dormant in many women. As Peggy Klaus, author of *Brag! The Art of Tooting Your Own Horn without Blowing It* says, "Women are less likely to draw attention to themselves and take ownership of their successes. They tend to attribute their accomplishments to other people, their families, or a work team. Don't sell yourself short by underestimating the value of what you do." She recommends taking ownership of your abilities by keeping a running list of things you've done.

━━━━━━━━━ *TRAILBLAZER* ━━━━━━━━━

Emily Warren Roebling (1843–1903)

Though her husband was credited as the Brooklyn Bridge's chief engineer, Emily played a major role in the bridge's construction. In 1883, she helped oversee the completion of the bridge after her husband became ill. She also was the first woman to address the American Society of Civil Engineers.

Telling people about your successes, in this case the Smart Risk you've taken, will not only impress them, it may put you at the top of their list when new opportunities arise. Confidence is contagious. Higher ups are more likely to believe in you if you believe in yourself. Don't let your achievements slip under the radar screen. Deb Traskell, a Senior Vice President at State Farm, advises, "There is nothing wrong with making sure that people value your work. I think women are a little shyer about approaching this, but the workplace is so fast-paced and hectic that unless you check in, people really might not know when you deserve credit."

These simple exercises will help you get practice in stating your wins. You may feel awkward doing them, but you are exercising a new muscle, and it will get easier in time.

Exercise 1

Go to a mirror. Now, look yourself straight in the eye and say your name, the Smart Risk you have taken, and what you have achieved or learned. Say it a few times with the deepest and most booming voice you have. I've used the mirror technique through-out my career. It helps me reconnect with my inner strength.

Exercise 2

This week, when you greet a friend, family member, or colleague and they ask, "How are you?" answer them in a casual way and then work into the conversation the risk you've taken and what you have achieved. Keep this short and to the point.

Tap into Women's Networks for Support

You want to keep reinforcing an assertive, more confident you—a woman who is a Smart Risk-Taker, open to advancing her life. If you are not a member of a business women's group, look for one at your company or seek out local associations in your area. These networks can provide you with an opportunity to exchange strate-gies with women at different levels of the organization. Joining with female colleagues can be both validating and informative.

In the last few years, I have witnessed the growth of corpo-rate women's groups across the country. Deniz Schildkraut is one of the co-founders, a charter member, and a past president of the Women's Forum of Kodak Employees (WFKE), a women's employee network at the company. She reveals, "My interactions with other members and company leaders have helped me develop confidence. I was able to make a major change in switch-ing departments. One of the keys to risk-taking is having a safety network—it's like a harness that supports you when you jump off a platform. Personal relationships are critical."

Pay It Forward

Share the wealth! What a wonderful concept. Yes, you will receive support by joining a network, but you'll also have the opportunity to share your expertise. As Margo Gray, President of Horizon Engineering Services Co., says, "Don't hold on to your knowledge. When someone helps you, you have to pay it forward. When you give back, you will always be taken care of." It's also been my experience that as I help other women exercise their potential, I further realize my own.

Develop a Trailblazer Mentality

By following the Six-Step Program, you have forged new ground—you are a trailblazer. Let's take a look at some of the practices that have helped women move ahead with conviction.

- **They are filled with gratitude:** Smart Risk-Takers follow-through and practice gratitude at each step of the way, no matter what transpires. Have you noticed how attractive that can be? Oprah Winfrey talks a lot about this and lives it first-hand.
- **They see the opportunity in challenging situations:** They are not deterred by the obstacles that come up. They believe that a Smart Risk should be pursued once they have identified it as a Best Bet, and take action, believing it can

be achieved. Ellen Swallow Richards, the first female to graduate from MIT, took the initiative to apply to this prestigious school even though no woman was accepted before her.

- **They know their priorities and act accordingly:** They do not get bogged down in minutia. They are focused on what is most important to achieve their goal and have the faith that they can go the distance. Valentina Tereshkova didn't let the rigorous qualification process of the Soviet space program deter her from persevering and becoming the first woman in outer space.

Quick Tips

- Review your risk-taking process. Look at what worked, what didn't, and how you will do things differently next time.
- Brag! Let people know about your accomplishments. This may feel uncomfortable at first, but the more you do it, the easier it will get.
- If you are not a member of a women's group or association, join one to share strategies and network.
- Develop a trailblazer mentality. Keep practicing the successful habits of women who are forging new ground.

POWER LINK: Go to www.womenworking.com/power_contacts/ contacts.php for a list of corporate women's groups, women's associations, and useful links.

DON'T STOP—
SUCCESS BREEDS SUCCESS

DECLARATION:

I experience my life as a constant progression.
I tap into my creativity and advance new goals.

QUALITIES OF A SMART RISK-TAKER:

Perseverance
Strength
Creativity

Smart women are risk-takers. They challenge the status quo,
being tenacious and having the courage to persevere
in a positive direction.

—Suzanne Danielle,
Talent Management Consultant

As you become a more experienced risk-taker, you take control of your destiny and use your power wisely. In our Six-Step Program, continuous action is crucial to positive change. You had a vision of what you wanted to achieve and, teamed with others, set about making it happen. Along the way, you practiced patience, remembering that risk-taking is a process. So many people stay stuck in a rut, confused, playing it safe, and afraid to make changes. But you didn't—you took a Smart Risk. Whether you achieved your goal or not, you are a winner because you launched out in a new way.

TRAILBLAZER

Elizabeth Robinson Schwartz (1911–1999)

At the 1928 Olympic Games in Amsterdam, Elizabeth became the first woman to win an Olympic gold medal in track and field. Overcoming injuries sustained in a 1931 plane crash, she earned a second gold medal in 1936.

Now that you've taken a Smart Risk, don't stop! You are in a prime position to experience a ripple effect. One woman from our Risk-Taking Survey acknowledged that taking risks is initially frightening, but the payoff is incalculable. She says, "All these experiences build on top of each other. It's amazing how knowledge learned in one area can be used in another." Knowing that you can take a Smart Risk and succeed establishes confidence to step out in new ways. Many women I interviewed for this book reported feeling more confident about taking risks after taking their first major one.

Yet all too often people face what I call the Plateau Mentality—an inertia that creeps in as they rest on their laurels. You must recognize the strides you have made, but this acknowledgment should also help you realize that you are capable of much more.

You're primed for action because you've been exercising your risk-taking muscle and should be thinking about your next Smart Risk. You must keep the ball rolling now that momentum is building.

Your New Business Goal

For those of you who are not pursuing a goal at the moment, you are about to choose a new one. Recall the method we used in Step One. It must be something that you feel passionate about, something that gets your juices going, that will help you stay focused and follow through.

Now set the wheels in motion. Declare your goal out loud—you are about to analyze the risk you are considering taking.

Next apply the Risk Quotient to determine if your goal is a Best Bet. Use the review charts that follow to do this. Analyze the pluses and the minuses of pursuing this goal. Remember to assign a weight to each entry. If you need to be refreshed on how to do this, reread Step Two.

My New Goal _____

_____

_____

YOUR RISK QUOTIENT BALANCE SHEET

+	**–**
Total:	**Total:**

Remember, Timing Is Everything

When considering whether your risk is a Best Bet, it's important to view it again in a larger context. Look at when the ideal time would be to take this risk, then compare it to where you are in your life now. Fill out the Career and Family Timelines and assess how taking this risk fits into your life. Does the ideal time line up with where you are presently?

CAREER TIMELINE

Ideal time

Entry into workforce   **Career peak**   **Retirement**

Entry into workforce   **Career peak**   **Retirement**
Actual time

FAMILY TIMELINE

Ideal time

Single   **Married with children**   **Other dependents/ elder parent(s)**

Single   **Married with children**   **Other dependents/ elder parent(s)**

Actual time

What About Your Other Priorities?

In considering whether you will take a risk, you need to look at your other priorities. Ask yourself, "If I pursue this goal at this time, will any of my other life goals be undermined? If so, which is the most important?" To gain clarity, fill out the Priorities chart.

YOUR PRIORITIES

If the pluses of taking the risk exceed the minuses, it's the right time in your life to pursue it, and if it doesn't rule out other priorities you value highly, then it's a Best Bet. (If the risk is a No Go, or a Not Now, go back to the drawing board and identify a new goal.) For Best Bets, proceed to the next step: mobilizing your team. Think of several people who can help move your efforts forward. Be specific as to what you need them to do and what's in it for them. When you are ready to take the leap, think about your past experiences and what you learned from them. Move forward with your thought-out plan, knowing that whatever happens you've done your best.

TRAILBLAZER

Ruth J. Simmons (1945–present)

One of her achievements as the president of Smith College was to start a program of engineering. In 2001, she became the first African American, male or female, to head an Ivy League institution when she assumed the presidency at Brown University.

Broadening Your Risk-Taking Experiences

We've identified business risks and have applied our Six-Step Program to them. Our method can also work in other areas of your life, from making small changes to your daily routine (like trying a new exercise class or taking a different type of vacation) or, on a more serious note, to looking at an investment with a financial adviser.

You can even use the Six-Step formula to gain clarity about a relationship. For example, for over a year Judy had been dating a man she met through business. She felt they weren't getting any closer, so she decided to have a heart-to-heart with her companion. What became apparent was that he was content with keeping things at the same level, whereas her priority was to be involved in a committed relationship. Judy was forced to make a decision: Was she ready to risk breaking up with him and start dating again? She worked her Risk Quotient with me, and she made the decision to move on. At this stage in her life, she didn't have time to give to a relationship that wasn't going anywhere.

Regarding finances, I've used the help of a financial adviser and an abbreviated Risk Quotient to guide my decision about what investments to pursue. For example, I work up a balance sheet of pluses and minuses of a particular investment—see which way the scale is tipped, look at the potential risk in relation to my needs at the moment, and make a decision.

Here's how Jennifer explored a financial opportunity that was presented to her. She's a mid-level manager at a large company and a single mother of an 8-year-old girl. Over the course of several years she managed to save about $20,000 that she put into a bank account. Jennifer's number one concern is to prepare for her daughter's college education. Her parents suggested that she move this money into investments to get a better rate of return. Although she wanted to "grow" the money, she felt this could be risky given the volatility of the stock market. With a financial adviser, she assessed the risk of moving her money into an investment portfolio.

When Jennifer filled out her Risk Quotient, there were an equal number of pros and cons. When she weighed what was most important, however, it was to increase the amount of money available for her daughter's college education. The best time for Jennifer to invest would be now, while her daughter is young and their expenses are not as high as they will be in the future. In order to offset the volatility of the market, which could work either positively or negatively, her financial adviser suggested a product where the principal was locked in so she would not lose her initial investment if anything happened. The potential return she would make on it was better than what she was getting now. She decided to move forward with the opportunity.

Take a moment to think about how you might use our Six-Step Program in other areas of your life. Where do you feel stuck? Where are you ready to make a change? Use the tools you learned in the first part of this book as a guide, and reach out for support when you need it. Continue living a life where you take Smart Risks!

TRAILBLAZER

Gertrude Ederle (1906–2003)

At just 19 years old, Gertrude became the first woman to swim the English Channel in 1926. She completed the challenge faster than any man before her, breaking the previous record by nearly two hours.

Quick Tips

- Don't get complacent. Be aware of the many opportunities around you to advance your business life. Keep Smart Risk-Taking on your radar screen.

- Use the Six-Step Program in your personal life. Reach out for support to help you make wise decisions.
- Pass it on. Offer your help to other women as they advance to a new level. The spirit of giving offers returns that can't be calculated.

POWER LINK: Visit womenworking.com/lifestyle to find expert advice on making changes in your personal life.

PART TWO

TRIUMPH WITH VICTORIOUS MENTORS

SUCCESSFUL WOMEN WHO TAKE SMART RISKS AND SHARE THEIR STORIES

On my 40th birthday, I quit my job at Nike and reorganized my work life into three pieces: (1) a business life, (2) a creative life, and (3) a public service life. That's the blend of work that I craved and believed would give me the balance I sought.

—Liz Dolan, Satellite Sisters

The women you are about to meet are trailblazers. They demonstrate courage, compassion, and intelligence. Each is a change agent in her own right. Let their stories support you as you launch out in new ways, taking Smart Risks when the timing is right. Like a ripple effect, your example will also empower others to explore the things they are passionate about.

DOLORES MORRIS

VICE PRESIDENT
HBO Family & Documentary Programming

Drawing from her background as a teacher in a theater arts
department, Dolores has dedicated her career to providing
first-rate family entertainment. Her love of children's
programming has led her to take Smart Risks rooted
in passion, intuition, and thought.

You need to go through challenges in your career in order to know who you are: how strong you are, how far you're willing to go for an idea, how hard you're willing to fight, and what you're willing to put up with. Working in family and children's programming, I've had an interesting challenge to tackle in that every project I commit to must be award-winning. Children's shows are at the bottom of a network's priorities because they don't make much money, so I always have to choose distinctive programming, things you won't see on any other network. This puts a unique pressure on me, but one that I've been able to meet thanks to doing a lot of homework, keeping on top of the competition, and staying committed to my purpose.

The passion I have for what I do motivates me to take big risks in programming because I believe in the projects I stand behind. I began my career as a teacher at an alternative school's theater arts department. Once I began producing children's plays and musicals there I knew I had found something I loved and wanted to do forever. I just needed to translate all this passion and energy into a long-term career. I was able to get my first job at the Children's Television Workshop (CTW) producing a science program called *321 Contact*. I wouldn't say I was lucky to get this position because I believe in being prepared for opportunity. I took that opportunity and kept seeking out other venues that would allow me to create one-of-a-kind, high-quality children's entertainment, working at several networks before my current job in the HBO Family Division. Ever since I started out as a teacher, I knew that education and entertainment are things I was born to do. Now I just have a larger classroom to play in.

I've learned to pick my battles when it comes to choosing projects. When I find something I believe in, I'll make sure there are other people whom I can form partnerships with to push for it. My favorite challenges are the biggest risks, the ones I've really had to decide, "This is the one I'm going to fight for," and then go in and say, "Trust me, let's do this."

The failure that comes with taking risks is a good thing, but you really have to think with each decision you make, "Should this project be tabled until a later time? Are the people involved going to trust me in the future if this project doesn't work out?"

I fought one of my biggest battles for a project that I felt strongly about. In the 1980s I worked for one of the large networks. I wanted to do a drunk driving special because I felt confident in the program's original script, all-star cast, and its potential to be a breakthrough presentation. For some reason, my boss at the time didn't care for the idea. At first I staged a tantrum in his office and said, "If you don't think this is a big issue, I'm going to go downstairs and have a couple of drinks." He took that as a good sign that I was going to let the issue go and leave him alone, but I added, "I'm going to go downstairs and have a few drinks and then I'm going to go uptown and get your child and drive him around the block." Shock value aside, he still wasn't affected by my campaign, so I began communicating with the network's media relations and community outreach staff. They informed me that the government was seeking out quality children's programming to promote in the wake of a growing trend of violent kids' cartoons. When the network head called my boss to ask if he had any ideas, he immediately suggested the drunk driving special. The program was produced and went on to win all sorts of awards.

I would never have been able to risk my reputation for these kinds of projects if I didn't always have a plan. Seventy-five percent of breaking through is knowing what's going on everywhere. There are so many new shows in the fall, but I watch everything. Even if shows are awful, I want to know what they're about. I want to know who's doing what because I need to have a working knowledge of everything that's happening. It's always changing and I find it fascinating but it's also crucial to succeeding. Nobody has time to tell you what they're doing. You're expected to come in knowing, and you wouldn't want to compromise relationships within your company or industry by not doing your homework.

The relationships I've formed with others in the industry have been crucial to my success. I carried with me the strength and support of my employers at previous jobs, who had seen my passion and taken the time to sit down with me to talk about my career. Those meetings really meant a lot to me because they advised me to roll with the punches and not give up. There is still very much a glass ceiling for women, and as a black woman I have always felt I need to be twice as good. But I've used this to my favor. I know what's expected of me, so I can do it and move on. For all of the challenging experiences I've had, I can now say that anything that happens in the future will be a piece of cake.

LOUISE FRANCESCONI

VICE PRESIDENT
Raytheon Company

PRESIDENT
Raytheon Missile Systems

As head of one of the largest missile-making enterprises in the world, Louise is a powerful example of what can happen when you embrace opportunity. Named one of Fortune's *50 Most Powerful Women, she began her ascent to the top by taking on unfamiliar roles.*

I believe I have a high tolerance for risk because I have a passion for change. I worked for Hughes Aircraft Company one summer during college and used my studies as an economics major to evaluate how inflation was affecting the defense industry. I realized how much the defense industry needed that kind of analysis at the time. The field was changing, and I was right in the middle of it. I've retained that enthusiasm for change at Raytheon.

The calculated risk that stands out most in my mind is when I moved out of a traditional and defined role as a CFO to take on

the newly created and undefined position as the deputy leader of
the Missile business. It was a job that would require me to expand
my technical knowledge of our programs and products—which
involves very complex engineering—and I would be charged with
running and growing the business. I made the change because I
wanted to broaden myself beyond my traditional finance role and
have others begin to see me in a different light. I had also gotten
very comfortable as CFO, which was a trigger to me that it was
time to push my learning by moving on. The timing was right
because I was already acting in a broader capacity than a typical
CFO, and therefore was an excellent candidate for the position.

On the personal side, my life was full of change and chaos. I
had just moved my family from California to Arizona and my
brother-in-law had been diagnosed with terminal cancer. My
husband and I made the decision that he would leave work to
provide full-time care for his brother and our young son.

When I took the deputy position, I was fortunate to have
tremendous support from my boss, my husband, and my family.
There were others—mostly technical folks—who were concerned that I was "getting out of my lane" and didn't have the
technical background for this broader business role. I'm glad I
didn't let them deter me because it turned out to be absolutely
the right move for me. Today I'm the president of the business,
and it's been a fantastic experience.

Learning is what excites me, and this role provided me
plenty of opportunity for that. One thing I've learned is that
when you know what you're good at, you can be good at many

jobs. For me that is leadership and managing large organizations, and those strengths have allowed me to be successful. I've also had good self-esteem. I think you only take risks if you have confidence in yourself, which is confirmed by success.

I would tell women who are hesitant about taking a risk that they need to understand if the risk fits their strengths. Risk for risk's sake is not my thing. If you want something really badly, you need to know your strengths and weaknesses, be willing to learn—often in very public settings—and be motivated by succeeding, no matter who or what stands in your way. But most importantly, take help and support willingly. You're going to need it!

SHEILA SCHECTMAN

CEO
Giftcorp, Inc.

A poster child for entrepreneurial success, Sheila turns ideas into reality. Relying on a combination of calculated risk-taking and shear perseverance, she has twice built profitable businesses from the ground up.

I grew up in a family that owned a home furnishings business. I'm also an identical twin; my sister is an entrepreneur and CEO of her own company. I guess I've always had merchant blood in me.

However, when I started out 25 years ago I planned to be a stay-at-home mom, with two young children to raise. But like many homemakers, I wanted something more. A friend and I decided to open up a high-end food emporium, which at that time was a new idea. We headed to the Big Apple and went directly to an established source for guidance. We practically knocked down the doors of Joel Dean and Giorgio Deluca (founders of Dean & Deluca), accosting them on the sidewalks of SoHo until they agreed to apprentice the two of us. For six months, they gave us an insider's view of the industry, and by 1981 we were ready to open our own gourmet food store.

In order to do this, we needed capital. We had a very sophisticated business plan, but were turned down by 10 banks. They didn't think we could make a go of it. We ended up getting start-up money from the Small Business Administration and created Nanshe's.

Twelve years later, I took some time off to stay home with my teenage daughters, but that plan only lasted two weeks before I had my sights set on another venture. This time, I did it solo. I started by making gift baskets in my basement at home. Within 10 years, I was shipping gifts nationwide from a 25,000-square-foot facility. In 2003, Gifted Expressions was launched, a spin-off company allowing women to sell Giftcorp gifts from their homes.

I have put a lot on the line, especially when I took my company national. I think risk is about two things—believing in yourself and surrounding yourself with a lot of good advisers. Risk has to be calculated. Ideas are wonderful, but converting them to successful operations is another story.

The other thing that's critical to launching your own business is truly having passion about what you do. I know that sounds like a fuzzy word that's overused, but I think that if entrepreneurs aren't passionate about what they're doing, they can forget about it. There's many a day when the passion's going to pull you through when nothing else does.

Lynn Laverty Elsenhans

EXECUTIVE VICE PRESIDENT,
GLOBAL MANUFACTURING
Shell Downstream Inc.

After earning an MBA from Harvard, Lynn found
herself uninspired by the financial sector, so she took an
unconventional leap into the male-dominated world of
manufacturing operations. Staying true to her goals,
she updates her knowledge base in preparation
for each new move.

I came to work for Shell right after getting an MBA from
Harvard. Although I have been with them ever since, my roles in
the company have evolved and changed as a result of the calculated risks I've taken.

I started working at Headquarters involved in strategic planning and competitive analysis. The traditional next step for an
MBA would be a financial position, but that didn't interest me as
much as operations. I had little experience in chemical or
mechanical engineering, the normal degree background required
for operations in the process industries, but I couldn't ignore my

passion to explore the manufacturing end of the business. I decided to take a job in a refinery, which was a big risk. For one thing, few women worked in operations at the time, so I risked some isolation. Second, the job required me to stay at the refinery for four years with no chance of promotion. My coworkers actually respected my move because it showed the commitment I had to my career and my resiliency to deal with difficult situations. I've never regretted my decision.

In 1998 I was faced with another big move when I was approached to relocate to Singapore to run Shell's refining and marketing business for the Middle East and Asia. Again I would be striking new ground because few Americans at Shell worked in that geographic area. But I saw this as an opportunity to become involved in the future of the industry, which I believed was in Asia. From both a personal and professional standpoint it was a risk worth taking, and I went for it.

With my husband remaining in Houston to tie up our affairs for the first few months of my relocation, I was alone in a completely new place. I noticed immediately that the values and conduct of the Singaporeans was dramatically different from mine. I was initially nervous about fitting in or effectively working in what I saw as a more rigid environment than I was used to.

My Asian colleagues had the potential for being great personal and professional coaches to me due to their strikingly different perspective. But I had to learn to communicate with them first. I realized that trying to impose my model of doing things on someone else was only going to frustrate them. It proved far more effective to understand where they were coming from because I realized that our business goals were more similar than they were different. Knowing this made it possible for us to achieve success.

I believe that pushing yourself to take a risk is a necessary part of life, but you need the proper knowledge and support to do so. Making informed decisions is liberating, but it also means taking responsibility for those decisions and their consequences. If you are prepared, you can confidently take risks. Confidence has worked for me in my career. The ability to project confidence and state what you want is what people expect of their leaders.

I always take stock each year and focus on my current situation. I ask myself whether I'm happy—do I still have some goals to accomplish. Then I set a timeline to take action toward my goals. Life is just too short to be miserable at any point. With my goals set out before me, I can consciously make a decision about my future. Having that sense of control makes me more satisfied that the risks I am taking will bring me what I want.

Margo Gray

PRESIDENT
Horizon Engineering Services Company

*Taking on an extremely large project was a risk for
Margo and her company, but they didn't put limits on their
potential. Accepting this $80 million assignment
led to the company's taking on more jobs of this scale,
which benefited the business and its employees.*

Looking back at how I got where I am today, I can say I've
never taken the conventional road to doing anything. I spent 17
years in law enforcement, which seemingly has nothing at all to
do with my current career in civil engineering. As one of the only
women in my unit, I came up against a lot, but I didn't look at
that as an impossible mountain to climb. I became the first
woman to apply to and pass Oklahoma's elite defensive tactics
instructor school, and went on to train over 5,000 officers to
fight and protect themselves. There are still doors for women to
open, so you cannot get stuck thinking things must always
remain how they are. It's like the story of the four-minute mile.
Everyone thought it would never be broken, but someone did it,

and then more and more people did. Someone has to keep breaking those records.

After the death of my father, I left my career in the police force so I could move closer to my mother, and I began working within my tribe, the Osage Nation. Some years later, I met my future business partners at a holiday party. I believe in faith—you are supposed to meet the people who come across your path. My friend introduced me to these two men, the owners of Horizon Engineering, out of happenstance. We began talking, and six months later we created a partnership. We looked at the work we could do in Indian Country, and the possibilities were amazing. Today we are doing phenomenal work that makes a difference. We are a part of building roads, bridges, and hospitals, and we also help improve community infrastructures by ultimately creating jobs. Depending on the assignment, we may stay in an area for up to two years, and our presence makes a profound impact as we hire people from the community and serve as mentors. We love what we do, and that contributes to our success.

Horizon wouldn't be where we are today as a business if we did not take well thought-out risks. I remember when we did our first $80 million project. It was in the gaming industry, a fast-paced world because, really, it's all about gambling. After accepting the deal and saying, "Yes, we can do it," I walked away and thought, "How am I going to do this?!" It was just something I hadn't done before, and in order to get it done, I just had to change my thinking. We were working with different deadlines, a different scope of work, but we took it on and grew as a result.

We had to break down that initial barrier in order to grow and expand. Since then, we've done numerous casinos. We could have just stuck to what we knew and maintained the status quo, but by expanding our market, our business and our employees benefited together.

Taking a risk in business is an everyday thing, but it must be done with forethought and caution. I went from working as an officer and making decisions in split seconds that would change people's lives forever to taking risks in a corporate setting that required caution. In law enforcement, I was dealing with safety, lives being saved, and situations where a gun could be involved, or an accident where seconds and minutes really counted. Dealing with people everyday like that, then going into this line of work makes taking risks easy for me. I just do it with more forethought. If you dream big, you can do whatever you want.

ANNA CATALANO

EXECUTIVE COACH & ENTREPRENEUR

After many years as a superb marketer in the oil industry,
Anna took a major leap and left the corporate world.
Drawing on her inner strength and courage to make the move,
she is redefining her goals with enthusiasm and passion.

By many accounts I should have been satisfied where I was. I was Group Vice President of Marketing for one of the largest firms in the United Kingdom. I was paid very well, living the enviable life of a U.S. expatriate in London, with two kids happily in school, and a stay-at-home husband who ran the household like clockwork. I accomplished all my goals there and made my mark, but there was no further growth for me. Leaving that world seemed a huge risk; I had never worked anywhere else, in any other industry, and didn't know whether I could find anything that could measure up to what I had.

When I shared the situation with my husband, my family, and a few friends that I was contemplating leaving, their support was unequivocal. They didn't tell me what to do or what not to do—they only made sure I thought through the issues with as much head as heart, and gave me the confidence that I'd do the right thing.

I realize now how important that support is during a time of career or life transition. Perhaps it's why many people choose not to make a change. They don't have the support they need to do it. Instead, they stay and make the best of things, only to have regrets later in life.

Between my resignation and the end of a five-month transition time, I didn't seek new employment, because, frankly, I wasn't sure what I wanted. I only knew not to jump into something quickly and to give myself time to reflect, recharge, and renew. After a period of time, I interviewed with several firms who offered only more of what I left behind—more travel, more money, and more stress.

I decided to build a non-executive portfolio and work as an executive coach and mentor, allowing me to do the things I enjoy most. I also embarked on the start of my own business, combining professional experience with personal passions. Most importantly, I enjoy spending more time with my family, an opportunity I will never compromise again.

I feel as though I have entered a new phase of my life, both professionally and personally. I have no regrets about spending over two decades in the corporate world. It made it possible for me to move into this new chapter. I was recently asked by a good friend to recap what I learned. I summarized it as follows:

Yesterday, I valued charisma and intelligence. Today, I value compassion and wisdom.

Yesterday, I spent a lot of time listening to advice from others. Today, I spend an equal amount of time hearing my own voice.

Yesterday, I was out to prove that I could be successful. Today, I want to spend more time enabling others to find their own success.

During this transition I've learned a lot about taking risks. Risk is not about the unknown; it's about the un-optimized. Our greatest risk is not discovering who we can become. The world needs all of us at our best and truest selves!

Jan Babiak

MANAGING PARTNER OF TECHNOLOGY
AND SECURITY RISK SERVICES
Ernst & Young LLP, U.K.

In 1997, Jan became one of the first women to run
a business unit at a large accounting firm.
While she admits that it is not always easy to be
a trailblazer, she accepts the challenge and continues
to take the road less traveled.

After over 20 years working for a global firm most noted for its accountants rather than its risk-takers, I am forced to smile when someone applies the stereotype of conservative businessperson to me. You see, I have

- Done lots of public speaking, which statistics show is most people's number one fear (with *death* as number two);
- Moved to and lived in a foreign country;
- Skied the black runs;
- Bungee jumped several times; and
- Sky dived more than 100 times.

145

In business I have taken risks as well. They haven't been the heralded risks of the entrepreneur who gives up everything for her dream, but rather risks taken by fearlessly forging a new diverse leadership model for the future. This has required uncompromising performance and determination, attempts at charm and good-natured humor, and taking well-articulated and robust challenges when required—all in an environment that was not naturally drawn to diversity.

On my journey, I have taken the road less traveled, forgoing predictable success in a well-defined business line in favor of creating a new business line, which could have, and nearly did at one point, destroy my reputation for uncompromising performance. Ultimately, the business line has surpassed everyone's wildest dreams, but I continue to learn along the way.

There are a few lessons I would share with another woman intrepid enough to brave the highest altitudes of the corporate ladder:

First, like many women, if you need to vent in order to stay sane, carefully consider to whom you vent. You need a safe, supportive, nonthreatening, and challenging person often found among senior women at your level in other organizations.

Second, there are some differences between men and women in the workplace. Work to understand rather than deny those differences, and then responsibly use that knowledge to great effect for you and your organization.

Third, sometimes the organization is not one that is willing to evolve. You then must assess the situation objectively, be brave, even ruthless, and act in your own long-term best inter-est. I don't know who said it first, but there's a great saying in the South: "If you're riding a wild horse, there is no way to get down gracefully!"

The road to equality is not yet finished and we all need to take responsibility, regardless of our age, experience, or gender to help level the playing field.

LYNN DAVENPORT

CLAIM TEAM MANAGER
State Farm

Navigating change isn't easy, but Lynn used an office consolidation as an opportunity to take stock of her options. Now settled in a new position, she exercises her risk-taking muscle in other areas of her life.

Several years ago, I managed an operation spanning across three different states, and my colleague was in charge of a similar territory. My company merged these two areas into one zone, and we were asked to come up with a consolidation plan. I recommended that my job be eliminated.

I wanted to approach this change in a positive manner and set a good example for my team, who were also struggling with the unknowns of office changes. I had been in the same position for eight years and had grown as much as I could in it—there was no real challenge anymore. I also knew the likelihood of obtaining the position over my highly capable colleague was very slim.

One of my mentors had said she would find a spot for me if I wanted to join her department. She supported me as well as other upper-level managers who were familiar with my work. My boss asked me to lead a temporary high-profile project for 18 months in the interim. I did take a position with my mentor's group, and I have since been able to bring a fresh perspective and new concepts to the department.

Handling transition has taught me many lessons. Stepping outside of my comfort zone is one of the best personal and professional growth experiences I've had. I've learned new processes and philosophies, yet have an opportunity to bring my talents to the table. My former employees have told me how they admired my courage and willingness to stick my neck out. They saw I survived a potentially horrendous situation and actually thrived as a result of it. That inspired them to take similar risks within their careers.

This big risk I took helped to jumpstart my taking actions on a regular basis, and I have taken other significant risks since. Pushing the envelope at the right time and place, for the right reasons, has helped me become a better leader and a stronger contributor to my company's success.

STEPHANIE MOORE

VICE PRESIDENT,
HUMAN RESOURCES

BP, Exploration & Production Technology

*Moving up the ranks at BP, Stephanie has taken
on new assignments with enthusiasm and a zest
for adventure. Her ability to ask for help as she
moved from place to place made these transitions
easier for both herself and her family.*

I grew up in a small town in Georgia and entered the oil
industry in search of a career where I could develop my talents
and skills. At BP, I've made numerous physical moves in order
to advance in my field, taking me to offices in Cleveland,
Houston, Anchorage, London, and Maryland.

With each promotion and move, I was able to reach out for
help, which made understanding differences in jobs a lot easier.
I took a risk by asking senior leaders for their time, something
I started calling "101" classes. I'd be sitting in a meeting, for
example, at an early point in a new position, and my coworkers
would reference terms or projects I didn't quite understand.

Outside of those meetings, I'd ask them to explain these things to me and they did.

While taking risks to relocate was beneficial to my career, I was always aware of how it would impact my personal life, especially as the single mother of two children. My family was uppermost in my mind when I was considering new options at work. The kids were 2 and 5 years old at the time of our first move from Cleveland to Texas, so there wasn't a big discussion there—they just went where their beds were. As they got older, however, I realized the importance of open communication. We started having family meetings once a week, exploring what was going on in our lives. I kept the dialogue open all the time, not just when we were moving. We learned to depend on each other's strengths. When the kids had a tough time fitting in at their new schools and I didn't know where the grocery store or dry cleaner was, having a promotion would not be enough to get us through. Before I made any decisions to relocate, I concentrated on the school systems they would have to switch into, and also weighed the availability of the support they would have. The situation had to be right. When I was working in Anchorage, Alaska, there was talk about switching me to England when my son was in his last year of high school. I didn't turn down any opportunities, but I made our needs clear. He graduated in June, and that July we were on an airplane.

With these transitions, I learned to tap into my inner resources. Just when I thought I could not do it or take any more, I found that I could. Those kinds of experiences teach you who you are and what you are made of. You learn to reach out in ways that perhaps you thought you couldn't, asking for help when you needed it. What's the worst they can do, say no? Sometimes we unknowingly construct imaginary boundaries that hold ourselves back. Just feel the fear and do it anyway.

SHEILA CLUFF

FOUNDER & OWNER
Fitness Inc., The Oaks at Ojai

*An internationally known fitness expert, Sheila turned her
love of exercise into a lucrative career. As the former host
of a popular fitness show, she capitalized on her media
exposure to promote other ventures, always remaining
true to her vision and staying ahead of the curve.*

In the late 1950s, I was single, living in Canada, and working
two full-time jobs. I was a high school physical education teacher
and the head pro of two skating clubs in Canada. At the same
time, I had started a little side business, a fitness company teaching adults something I created called cardiovascular dance. I
found myself at a crossroads. I wasn't unhappy in my career, but
the joy of helping people feel better about themselves through
exercise was powerful. I also had a hunch that the fitness program
I had started would catch on.

In 1960, I made the decision to leave my steady income
behind, move to New York, and build Fitness Inc., the business I
still own and believe in today. I suppose I could have gone on

doing what I was doing and let my cardio dance business grow at its own pace—or not at all. But I believed in this product to the degree that I was willing to gamble everything on it, including my entire life savings. I sunk the whole nest egg on my idea.

In 1977, I took another calculated risk to expand my vision even further by leaving New York. I soon enjoyed widespread media exposure through a television show I hosted that served to publicize Fitness Inc. I also opened the Oaks at Ojai, one of California's first fitness destination spas, at a time when massages and facials were not yet mainstream. It was simply ahead of its time. Today, the Oaks has been in business for nearly 30 years and I have achieved great financial success.

My husband, whom I married shortly after launching Fitness Inc., was paramount to my success. During the early days of owning and operating the Oaks, he was willing to be the sole financial provider for me and our four children during the lean times when we worried about making payroll and rent. He also stood by me while I bucked societal norms. In those days, it was socially risky to work outside the home as a woman, and there I was starting a business!

Through it all, I learned that it's not easy to pursue your dreams. You have to have such a passion and belief in your product and the courage to hold the line in scary times. I had to become emotionally stronger and learn that I possessed strength I never knew I had. I was asked to give talks to other aspiring business owners, but I thought I wasn't credible because I didn't have a business degree. I was so wrong. Now I regularly speak to groups sometimes as large as 2,000 people with great comfort and ease. For those aspiring business owners, if you're going to start your own company, you can't dangle your toe in the water. You have to jump all the way in and swim as hard as you can. In doing this, it is also essential to create and maintain a balance in your life physically, emotionally, and creatively.

Linda Srere

BOARD DIRECTOR
Electronic Arts, Inc.,
Universal Technical Institute, Inc.
and aQuantive, Inc.

*Early experiences taught Linda to be true to what she
believed and were responsible for her rapid climb up the
corporate ladder. She puts a premium on being authentic
and takes Smart Risks when the timing is right.*

The biggest risk I think I ever took was early on when I was at
Ogilvy & Mather, an advertising agency. I was asked to give a
presentation on a new product that was scheduled to launch
nationally after an extended and very costly test market period.
The only hitch was that our interpretation of the data indicated
that the product might fail at a very high cost to the client. Of
course, no one wanted to hear that news. It was a case of telling
the Emperor he wasn't wearing any clothes.

I was only 26 years old, but my pitch to kill the product was
approved, and I presented it to the senior management of Ogilvy
& Mather as well as to the client. I'm sure I was chosen to make

the presentation because I was new and young, and if the client disagreed, I was a person who could be sacrificed to the "god of new products."

I knew that everything I said was supported by the data, but I still rehearsed my presentation and studied everything I could about the product, category, and test markets so that I could answer all questions. There's a way of saying to the client, "This is *your* product. At the end, it's *your* decision and we support it, but you have asked us for a point of view." You express your point of view, but you communicate that you're also part of the team.

In the long run, the client didn't introduce the product. They realized it was a mistake.

This risk had a profound impact on my career because there were people at both Ogilvy & Mather and at the client company who saw that, although young, I had the intelligence and strategic insight to understand what the problems were with this product and also the courage to represent my point of view. If we had endorsed the product and it had failed, I would have been shipped off to a very small assignment in Antarctica. Instead, the tough risk I took ended up being the right decision. I had the backing of the team by the time I made the presentation, and I then received recognition from influential senior people who helped guide my career.

When you're preparing for something like this, whether it's a big presentation or a small meeting, you have to write down your own notes and rehearse in front of a mirror—whatever helps. I have a habit of rehearsing my presentations while I walk to work. If I have a big meeting, I actually talk to myself, going over my point of view and facts verbally. I whisper to myself like a crazy person! But I'm using that time to focus and think about my presentation. I rehearse it so I am confident in my own voice.

I always enlist a team so that I'm not missing anything. It's very important that you don't work as a lone ranger and instead have a group of counselors that can say, "Here's what I see. What do you see?" Most often, they will help strengthen your point of view or offer a new perspective or insight that you might not have identified on your own.

Risks make you think of the road not taken. Maybe my life could have been different. Maybe my life would have been more fulfilling. I don't know. What I *do* know is that I thought very carefully about all the decisions and changes that I made. I've learned that all decisions carry consequences and take you in directions that you could never have imagined.

I continued to take risks in my life. I left the comfort of the business world that I loved to live in the Southwest. After 26 years spent working on airplanes, making presentations, and suffering from sleep deprivation, I felt it was time to live the life I had always imagined. This life now involves practicing yoga, competing in horse jumping, and even the occasional game of golf. I also maintain my connection to the business world by serving on three corporate boards.

I don't pretend to know where I'll be or what I'll be doing in the far, or even immediate, future, but I know that the following chapters of my life will involve taking risks of the mind and of the heart.

DENISE MORRISON

PRESIDENT

Campbell USA

*Advancing through jobs at Procter & Gamble, Nestle,
Nabisco, and Kraft, Denise learned early on to face her fears
and move forward anyway. Now as president of a large
division she has been named by* Fortune *as one of the
Most Powerful Women in Business.*

I've found that I've taken risks more often than not in my career
because I'm constantly pushing myself to grow, learn, and contribute. My experience in sales and marketing at Procter &
Gamble, Nestle, Nabisco, and Kraft established a firm foundation
for my current position at Campbell's. Of course it's always unset-
tling to move to another company or to another division, but it is
like the analogy of buying new shoes. The old pair is always more
comfortable. When you buy a new pair you may get some blisters
at first, but eventually you break them in and it feels good. Any
new position requires the leveraging of old skills along with learning new ones. Often, the talents that advanced you to your current
level are not necessarily the ones that will keep you there.

Trust is a key ingredient in taking risks in your career, and trust is formed by building credibility. First, you have to back up your opinion with facts. By nature I'm someone who collects a lot of information in order make an informed decision. Although I don't get bogged down with analysis, I believe that to have sound judgment you need to translate data into actionable insights in order to deliver positive results. This helps build credibility. You also need to establish relationships of trust to be considered for a big move. As part of these relationships, it is important to influence others while also listening to their input, rather than telling them what to do. Solid relationships built on good communication will help create a positive situation when faced with risk.

I make it my job to connect with other men and women in business to share my experiences as well as to gain insight from theirs. The risks I've taken in the past have given me a lot of insight to impart. At Nestle, I was asked to move from New York to Bakersfield, California as a VP of Marketing and Sales to administer the conversion of a manufacturing plant into a business with a full P&L. In addition to the uncertainty of relocating to another state, the action was a risk because the plant was losing a significant amount of profit. I saw this risk as an opportunity to turn a struggling business venture around. I sought other people's advice to compare perspectives and assess the situation. My desire to improve the business led me to take on the challenge. It was so rewarding when the business was profitable only two years later. I'm not afraid to put my neck on the line, but I'm not reckless about it. If I can see the possibility of a successful outcome, I'll go for it!

In taking calculated risks, it's all about taking the fear out of the action by looking at it in the context of skill building. In order to do this, I encourage others to go through a self-assessment to determine what skills they have and what skills they need in order to pursue their desired career track. Many people have a strong fear of failure. I do think it's important to understand that we all make mistakes and you can build your character by learning from them. I get up every morning in learning mode, and it just makes work so much more rewarding when I'm continuously growing, improving, and contributing.

STEPHANIE BURNS

PRESIDENT & CEO
Dow Corning Corporation

Rather than allowing fear to prevent her from taking on new roles, Stephanie has taken positions outside her area of expertise to expand her knowledge base—and it's paid off! This attitude has advanced her through the ranks, from researcher to CEO.

I had a strong interest in math and science growing up. My father, an English professor and academic dean, encouraged me to pursue it professionally. I completed a doctorate in chemistry and then joined Dow Corning's Research and Development group. Because I was so passionate about the advancement of science, this suited me perfectly. So I was, understandably, a bit apprehensive when I was encouraged to accept my first position outside of the laboratory. Even years later, when offered the post of Executive Vice President at Dow Corning, I remember thinking about this as a risk, wondering if I really had the full complement of skills to lead an entire organization. I couldn't imagine what I know now—that my scientific background and business experience would enhance my efficiency and decision making in the leadership roles ahead.

It's fantastic to think of how much learning has taken place on the job for me. As CEO, I've enhanced my financial and communication skills, and still use my technical background. It was gratifying to learn that, once established, we tend not to lose many skills. Our minds are amazing in that we just keep adding and adding to our mental portfolios.

This is how I make the case for encouraging others to take those opportunities that expand them professionally and broaden their expertise. If you're a little bored in your current career, then you've waited too long. Even within one company there are lots of ways to apply yourself. Every experience adds to your insights and value. For example, choosing to spend a year in France after completing my doctorate, and later in my career taking an assignment with Dow Corning in Brussels gave me perspectives on cultural diversity that I have found invaluable in leading in an increasingly global marketplace. Taking on the role of Director of Women's Health several years ago also pushed me to see things from a new perspective and foster relationships outside of the company, which continue to help me today.

Twenty years ago, when I was completing my advanced studies in chemistry, women were clearly in the minority. Today there are more women than men getting degrees in chemistry. Young women have more mobility in their careers now and they don't hesitate to change positions, companies, or careers. This is a good sign that risk-taking is becoming more commonplace for women.

I think women tend to feel pressure to be perfect at what we do. Men seem to be more comfortable taking risks and showing more of an, "I can do it, I can do anything," attitude. But women are sometimes held back (or hold themselves back) by the need to be fully skilled in an area before taking on the responsibility. We trap ourselves by being concerned that if we aren't the absolute best at something from day one, we won't get recognition and stay ahead. On the contrary, as long as we're stretching ourselves and learning, then we're on the right track.

It's so important to keep fostering this can-do attitude in working women and soon-to-be working women through mentoring and education programs. In addition to my husband, who has been a fantastic support all along the way, I've found that the most effective male mentors for me are the ones who have daughters themselves. They want and encourage their own children to have professional careers, and so they are conscious of and sympathetic to the fact that women in the workforce are still not always treated fairly. I look at my daughter, now the mother of two children, and I see someone successfully balancing her professional life and her family. I want to see the next generation of young women grow up with that same confidence in themselves and their careers. I've been working with the American Chemistry Society to develop children's math and science books that include women, because we are seeing young girls' interest and confidence in their math and science skills begin to wane once they hit middle school and high school. I feel fortunate to have so many opportunities to reach out to women in the field to try to reverse this trend.

A single career can take so many directions, so I remind women (and men) to be flexible and adjust to what they need at the moment to achieve balance. There isn't one equation for balance that will fit an entire career timeline. Life changes, careers change. Women have great adaptation skills. We must, fairly regularly, shift and redirect resources to manage all that life has to offer—career included. The people who are best at this do it while maintaining the most important foundation for contributions at work or anywhere—the essence of who they are and what they believe, as rooted in their core values.

Be true to yourself. Unwavering. Then, when opportunity "threatens" to pluck you out of your comfort zone and plunge you into new territory, you can pursue it without fear. You can have the confidence to apply your experiences, the patience to learn new skills, and the courage to take career risks that make contributions.

MIRIAM VIALIZ-BRIGGS

VICE PRESIDENT, MARKETING
IBM, Systems & Technology Group

Miriam has traded familiarity for the unknown throughout her career. She believes that taking risks is an act of collaboration, and puts a premium on relationships built on trust. With that behind her, she can jump in when the offer is right!

Learning a discipline can get you very far in your career, but the learning process is never over. Having studied Sociology as an undergraduate student, I entered business school with no corporate experience. Fortunately, I was offered a marketing fellowship in one of the business divisions of General Foods Corporation as part of my MBA, and this set my course. In many cases, one joins a large company and then goes on to either an equally sized corporation or a smaller one. In my case, I've gone in succession to larger ones. My subsequent moves from General Foods to American Express and finally to IBM seemed risky each time, but I wasn't hired for my knowledge of finance or technology (which I didn't have then). They hired me because I knew how to market, and marketing comprises many of the same disciplines no matter what the product or service. Of course, any time you change work environments there is a big sense of the unknown—will I like the way the company is run, or will I get along with the new people? But in order to move forward in my career I've had to develop my ability to connect quickly with a lot of people.

Whether it was for personal or professional reasons, the risk of leaving the familiarity of a good job behind has always been worth taking. At IBM, I now have the chance to work with the most phenomenal people, a host of brilliant scientists, researchers, and engineers from around the world. They've been willing to teach me about new and existing developments, and in this time of changing and competing technologies, I've found it very exciting to be a part of the organization. None of my roles before IBM were global either, so while I was forced to learn new ways of communicating with people from many cultures, I was also able to use my Hispanic background and multicultural experience to collaborate with a diverse group of teams.

Taking risks is not an individual enterprise. As with any business transaction, it relies on collaboration. As much as I feel that I have taken risks to constantly move forward in my career, I also feel that I couldn't have done so without relationships of trust, without people willing to support the changes I was making. IBM in particular has taken a lot of risks when they put me in different assignments, making me the chief marketing officer of several businesses and promoting me up to senior leadership. Of course I do my part and stay ahead of the competitive curve by keeping up to speed with what's going on, but I like to take risks to support others in return. A few years ago I was in charge of a new project and had to bring four people on board to join my team. I went out and did the recruiting myself, ultimately selecting people from different areas of the company whom I had never worked with before. I knew I was taking a risk by not knowing about their performance firsthand, but their diverse skills were crucial to the assignment ahead. They ended up being terrific additions and brought valuable perspectives to the work. I've learned that going for comfort will rarely bring you the breakthrough thinking you need in business.

With 25 years of experience, I find that I'm personally at a crossroads, but I'm looking forward to mapping out my next step. I feel that I've mastered the discipline of marketing by expanding my roles as I've changed companies, so I'm now considering branching out into other areas of IBM. I'm constantly looking for opportunities to get involved in activities outside my day-to-day role. Recently I began a speaking seminar that helps men and women learn how to become known in the marketplace. Through those seminars and through one-on-one mentoring, I emphasize the importance of marketing yourself. By forming relationships and making connections with people in different departments, or even with people outside your company, you stretch your abilities and also get to meet new people. For instance, by cochairing the marketing team for an open Grid computing nonprofit organization on a volunteer basis, I've been in contact with people I never would have connected with in my company, which enriches the work I do in my career.

Shaunna's success comes from a willingness not to play it safe. She believes that failure is a part of life, and when you view it in the right way, it can only make you stronger.

I grew up moving every couple of years both in the United States and overseas. My parents were always looking for the next adventure, whether it was traveling the back routes of India or moving to Australia. When you travel like that, you grow up with the notion that change is normal. In my career, I have changed positions approximately every two to three years, and usually to another turnaround or start-up situation. The first career risk I made was when I was 28. I was a high school English teacher and really enjoyed it, but I could not see myself in the classroom for the next 25 years. I had always been good at math and science and the idea of engineering came to mind. My husband, who was in dental school at the time, suggested that I take some engineering classes at night. I took his advice, and when he finished dental school I quit teaching and became a full-time student in mechanical engineering. When I returned to school in the early 1980s, I also chose to begin a family. I believe I was the first pregnant engineer the university ever had to deal with.

After graduating, I went to work for Texas Instruments. At my 15-year anniversary mark, I was running a worldwide division in a job I loved. Unexpectedly I was asked by the senior vice president of worldwide manufacturing to take over a plant that was on the brink of being shut down. I had never managed a manufacturing plant before, and it was fairly clear that if I wasn't successful in this job it would be somewhat career limiting. For me to go in as a VP and not be able to deliver was extremely high risk, and I actually said no two or three times. Nevertheless, when I considered the job I saw 1,400 people who wanted to succeed on TI's behalf. They just needed a leader and management team who could help them succeed together. I felt called to the job.

Once my acceptance was announced, there was some friendly and not so friendly betting on whether or not I would last six months. That was almost five years ago. The plant has turned around and a lot of good people have been able to contribute to TI in ways they never knew were possible.

I have always had coaches and mentors in my life who were committed to my success. A mentor early in my career told me, "When you face moments when you can't believe in yourself, believe in the people who believe in you." Having the faith and encouragement of people I respect and trust has allowed me to take risks in my life. You've got to have a heck of a support system. You will have those moments of darkness, of feeling overwhelmed and not competent. I would never have made it during the first two years of my current job if I didn't have that circle of support picking me up or holding me accountable when I needed it.

If I hadn't taken any risks, I never would have found out what my potential is. By creating a self-limiting world that appears safe, you're really wasting your talent. What we perceive as risky is usually just in our heads. I like to ask the question, "Is this going to be fatal?" Ninety-nine percent of the time, it's not. You may fail, no doubt about it, but I don't believe great organizations or people are great because they have avoided failure. They stand up to it. And when they do fail, they take ownership, learn, and get stronger from it. If you think in those terms, risk becomes a much easier leap to take.

Joyce Roché

PRESIDENT & CEO
Girls Inc.

*Never one to sit still, Joyce has constantly pushed herself
to step out of her comfort zone. With a career that spans
both the corporate and nonprofit arenas, she has been
an agent of change for both women and girls.*

I had been with Avon for five and a half years. It was my first marketing job, and I'd done very well. I'd moved up rapidly in the corporation, before being recruited to another cosmetics company as Director of Marketing. I didn't know if I could do marketing in a retail environment, and unlike Avon, this company did not have the greatest reputation in terms of its employee relationships.

Despite that, I knew if I didn't take the risk of going to a company known for having a very tough environment at this time in my life, I would probably never take the risk of challenging myself in retail marketing. I decided to do it because it was important to push myself in that way.

After two years, I was recruited back to Avon. At the time, the company was trying to change its marketing organization and wanted me to come and help. There was also the potential of becoming an officer in a short period of time. I went back because I felt like I had learned a great deal and had been able to prove to myself that I could really handle marketing in a tough retail environment. I returned to Avon, became a group officer, and, after 13 years, was heading Global Marketing. However, it started to look like that position would become a staff job (rather than a position with more advancement opportunities), so I knew I would need something different to keep me motivated and stimulated.

My next major risk was when I decided to leave Avon again. I took the experience that I had and said, "I'm going to go and find something that will be a new challenge for me." I left without a job, and it shocked everyone. Nobody really believed I was going to do this. It was a wonderful time. I got a lot of calls about a lot of different opportunities in a lot of different industries—telecommunications, retailing, etc.

One of those calls was from an investor group that was in the process of buying a small company in Savannah, Georgia, and they were changing the management. I had the opportunity of going in as the Executive VP of Global Marketing, but with the promise of becoming the president in a short time. So, after about six months, I decided to take the offer, and moved out of New York, down to Savannah to work for Carson Products, a top ethnic hair and beauty corporation. In about 10 months, I became president. We took the company public in Johannesburg and in the United States, faced a lot of challenges, and learned how to deal directly with Wall Street. After about four years, I decided that it was time to leave.

In the process of looking at other opportunities, I was doing some consulting for both profit and not-for-profit entities. I realized that I was rediscovering my passion in the work that I was doing with nonprofits. Just as I was about to take another corporate job, an opportunity with Girls Inc. opened up, and it just fit. I could work with women and girls in education, which was something I'd always been interested in. I did some soul-searching as a final check, and decided that I was going to take another big risk, and that was to move from corporate into non-profit. It's been almost five years now, and it's been a fabulous, fabulous transition.

JUDITH SHAPIRO

PRESIDENT
Barnard College

You need to do things that correspond to your own
personal integrity, and that philosophy has guided every risk
Judith has taken throughout her career.

A lot of the big decisions we make in life are made viscerally. I've often gotten myself out of situations because they just didn't feel right. After graduating from Brandeis University as a history major, I decided to go on in history at Berkeley. After three weeks, though, I knew I did not want to become a historian, so I went back to New York and applied to graduate schools. I had never taken a single anthropology course as an undergraduate, but the first anthropology book I ever read—Claude Levi-Strauss's *Tristes Tropiques*—was so beautiful that with no experience whatsoever I dropped myself into anthropology at Columbia's graduate school.

After graduating, I went heroically off doing fieldwork in a very inaccessible part of the Brazilian forest. That was risky in many ways, but I went for the intellectual adventure of working with the largest indigenous society in lowland South America that was still relatively isolated from outside contact. It was psychologically difficult to be there and do good research, but I would not change that experience. Being in a place like that is never going to be available to anyone again.

In 1970, I was the first woman ever appointed to what was then generally viewed as the strongest anthropology department in the country at the University of Chicago. It was an incredibly challenging and overwhelming experience. There were almost no women on the university faculty at that time, and I moved into an office that was vacated by perhaps the most famous anthropologist of all, Clifford Geertz. I felt totally and utterly inadequate. I hung in there, however, and after four years I was reappointed to a second term as an assistant professor.

Instead of staying at Chicago, I decided to leave this excellent research university for a liberal arts college—which at the time was probably viewed by most as a professionally risky move. I joined Bryn Mawr College in 1975 as Assistant Professor and rose through the ranks to become Chair of the Anthropology Department in 1982. After almost 10 years on the faculty, I made what might seem an unusual career decision and joined the college's administration to become the Acting Dean for a year. I had no intention of going into administration, but it turned out to be one of the best decisions of my life. Bryn Mawr provided me with an in-depth introduction to the world of women's colleges.

After a year as an Acting Dean, I became Bryn Mawr's first provost, a position I held for eight years. The next likely progression was college president. I wasn't sure if that was where I saw myself, but when the presidency opened up at Barnard College, I accepted it with great enthusiasm.

I had a tenured position at Bryn Mawr, and I could have been concerned about giving up that job security. I did not consider it appropriate to expect tenure at Barnard and I did not request it. This may have been risky, but my decision came out of confidence. I knew that if it didn't work out, there were other things I could do. For much of my life, I used to obsess over decisions, worry afterward about whether I had done the right thing, fret over past mistakes. Over time I have learned to take a more productive approach, learning from failure (which is a great teacher), focusing on how to fix what went wrong, and moving on. The essential point is to maintain a sense of personal integrity, to know that I have done my best. That is, for me, the home base that allows me to take risks worth taking.

Appendix

Women and Risk-Taking Survey: An unscientific online mail survey conducted in July 2005 with some of womenworking. com's Member Network

What is your industry?

Industry	Response Percentages
Arts	2.0%
Communications	3.7%
Consulting	3.3%
Education	4.0%
Engineering	5.6%
Finance	11.3%
Government	2.7%
Healthcare	4.0%
Hospitality	1.7%
Human Resources	2.3%
Information Technology	9.6%
Insurance	19.3%
Law	2.0%
Marketing	3.3%

(Continued)

(Continued)

Industry	Response Percentages
Sales	4.3%
Telecommunications	1.0%
Other	19.9%

Regarding your career, which of the following describes your position?

Position	Response Percentages
Entry Level	13.3%
Middle Management	44.9%
Senior Level Management	15%
Other	26.9%

Are you satisfied with your current career?

Response	Response Percentages
Generally satisfied, although there are a few aspects of my job that could be improved	68.4%
Occasionally satisfied, but there are many other career options that seem better to me	24.5%
Generally unsatisfied with my job	7.1%

If not satisfied with your career, why? (Check all that apply.)

Response	Response Percentages
Inadequate monetary compensation	32.6%
Unfulfilling, boring; I feel that I'm stagnating	38.4%
I am overworked, with not enough time to spend with family or friends	34.3%
There are other passions of mine that are more compelling	43.6%
Hostile or unsatisfactory work environment	16.9%
Lack of upward mobility	43.0%
My job is not in alignment with my values and beliefs	11.6%
Other	11.6%

Do you plan to change your current situation?

Response	Response Percentages
Yes, I am currently working on the change	38.7%
Maybe sometime in the future	35.9%
Probably not	13.6%
Definitely not; I have no plans to change my current situation	11.8%

How do you view risk-taking in relation to your career?

Response	Response Percentages
I welcome risks as opportunities to expand my experience and to grow	51.9%
Occasionally I shy away from taking big risks	30.2%
I take risks but rarely feel comfortable doing so	12.7%
I generally avoid taking risks	5.2%

When have you backed down from taking risks in the past? (Check all that apply.)

Response	Response Percentages
I assessed the pros and cons of taking the risk and realized there were too many uncertain factors at the time	53.6%
The idea of taking the risk scared me too much	17.2%
I had too much going on in my life to concentrate on making any big changes	38.7%
I knew that even if I followed through and took action, it wouldn't really change my situation	9.5%
I generally follow through when taking risks	31.0%
Other	5.1%

How do you define the word *risk*?

Response	Response percentages
A necessary yet uncertain step toward change	85.1%
An action that is likely to fail	1.0%
A rash decision made with little forethought	1.4%
Other	12.5%

Do you think there is a difference between men and women in relation to risk-taking?

Response	Response Percentages
No, everyone encounters challenging decisions and feels a certain amount of discomfort regarding taking risks	36.5%
Yes, women have it harder when it comes to initiating big changes and taking risks	50.4%
Other	13.1%

Why might women in particular have a hard time taking risks in their careers? (Check all that apply.)

Response	Response Percentages
Women have too many people depending on them to take uncertain actions	40.8%

(Continued)

(Continued)

Response	Response Percentages
Women may have been encouraged growing up to be agreeable and submissive rather than be assertive and take action	67.4%
I don't think women in particular have a hard time taking risks	17.4%
Other	12.1%

Which risk-taking strategies have you found to be most successful? (Check all that apply.)

Response	Response Percentages
Planning before making the change	84.6%
Gathering the support and feedback of others before I take a risk	66.3%
Waiting to see if my desire for change persists before actually taking a leap in a new direction	29.7%
Trusting my gut instinct and disregarding the opinions or criticism of others	48.0%
Other	5.4%

What additional factors have helped you take calculated risks? (Check all that apply.)

Response	Response Percentages
Good communication with others	71.2%
Staying focused	74.1%
Prioritizing action steps	67.6%
Being able to relax	30.6%
Depending on inner strength	67.6%
Other	8.3%

In what area(s) of your personal life do you take the most risks? (Check all that apply.)

Response	Response Percentages
Existing friendships and making new friends	38.2%
Networking	37.1%
Dating	7.6%
Child-rearing	12.0%
Interactions with spouse/partner	23.3%
Trying new things (i.e., exercise classes, travel, etc.)	76.4%
Other	8.0%

In what area(s) of your finances do you take the most risks? (Check all that apply.)

Response	Response Percentages
Long-term investing	43.4%
Shopping and purchasing smaller items such as clothing or jewelry	46.9%
Purchasing or renting a car	18.8%
Purchasing or renting a house or apartment	26.6%
Other	10.5%

INDEX

Additional information. *See*
www.womenworking.com
Affirming thoughts, 16–18
Agassiz, Elizabeth Cabot Cary, 42
Alliances/advisers. *See* Risk-taking
network
Alvarado, Linda G., 89

Babiak, Jan, 145–147
Ball, Lucille, 19
Bancroft, Ann, 63
Bellinger, Patti, 64
Benefit evaluation model, 25–29
Best Bet, xxi, 33, 35, 48, 113
Biographical sketches
Babiak, Jan, 145–147
Burns, Stephanie, 167–170
Catalano, Anna, 141–143
Cluff, Sheila, 155–157
Davenport, Lynn, 149–150
Elsenhans, Lynn Laverty,
133–135
Francesconi, Louise, 127–129
Gray, Margo, 137–139
Moore, Stephanie, 151–153
Morris, Dolores, 123–126
Morrison, Denise, 163–165
Roché, Joyce, 179–181
Schectman, Sheila, 131–132
Shapiro, Judith, 183–185
Sowell, Shaunna, 175–177
Srere, Linda, 159–161
Vializ-Briggs, Miriam, 171–173

Boit, Elizabeth, 69
Book website. *See* www.womenwork
ing.com
*Brag! The Art of Tooting Your Own
Horn without Blowing It*
(Klaus), 102
Bragging, 102–104
Bungee jumping, 35–36
Burns, Stephanie, 167–170
Business women's groups, 104

Career timeline, 43, 44, 112
Career-Vision list, 23, 24, 27–29
Catalano, Anna, 141–143
Clark, Celeste, 76
Cluff, Sheila, 155–157
Communication strategy, 76–77
Competitive edge, 74–77
Confidence, 103
Contacting a potential prospect,
68–72
Contingency plans, 57
Continuous action, 107–117
Cooper, Carla, 20
Corporate women's groups, 104
Courage, 83
Cowden, Barbara, 6
Creative Expansions, Inc. (CEI), 65,
199
Crump, Diane, 72

Danielle, Suzanne, 109
Davenport, Lynn, 149–150

De-clutter your mind, 92–95
Defeatist thoughts, 15–17
Dolan, Liz, 121

Ederle, Gertrude, 116
Elsenhans, Lynn Laverty, 133–135
Eng, Phoebe, 61

Family timeline, 43, 44, 112
Fear, 9–15
Feedback, 64–65
Feel the Fear And Do It Anyway
        (Jeffers), 9–10
Financial opportunity, 115–116
Focus, 74–76
Follow-through, 81–84
Forward thinking, 16–18
Francesconi, Louise, 63, 127–129
Friedman, David, 16

Gloeckler, Michelle, 83
Goal-setting, 18–29, 110–113
Goldman, Jess Alpert, 5
Graciousness, 72
Gray, Margo, 105, 137–139
Griffith, Ellen, 81
Guinier, Lani, 10–11
Gut sense, 46–48

Hare, 50
Homework, 71
Hutson, Nancy, 74–75

"If that should happen" plan, 57
Inner guidance, 47–48
Inner strength, 81–82
Interests, 7–8
Intimate relationships, 114–115
Inventory chart, 25–26

Jeffers, Susan, 9–10
Jones, Rochelle, 95

Kavovit, Barbara, 99
Klaus, Peggy, 102
Kreutzer, Ginger, 51

Lerner, Helene, 199–201
Limiting thoughts, 15–17
Lin, Maya, 82

Martinez, Annette, 54
Member Network survey. *See* Risk-
        Taking Survey
Memories, successful risk-taking
        experiences, 8–9
Menin, Julie, 47
Mentoring up, 73
Mentors, 119–186
Miller, Gail Sussman, 33
Mind clutter, 92–95
Mind clutter inventory, 92–94
Mind-talk, 15–18
Mink, Patsy Takemoto, 100
Mistakes, 83
Moderate (personality type), 87,
        90–91
Moore, Stephanie, 151–153
Morris, Dolores, 123–126
Morrison, Denise, 163–165
Mulcahy, Anne, 61

Network
    member (womenworking.com),
        96
    risk-taking, 59–78. *See also*
        Risk–taking network
    support, 104–105
New business goal, 110–113

No Go, xxi, 35, 48, 57, 113
Not Now, xxi, 35, 48, 57, 113

Ochoa, Ellen, 8

Passion, 6–8, 110
Past mistakes, 83
Pay it forward, 105
Perfectionism, 87–88
Perkins, Frances, 65
Personal life, 114–116
Personal stories. *See* Biographical
    sketches
Personal successful risk-taking expe-
    riences, 8–9
Personality type quiz, 84–87
Pessimistic thinking, 15–17
Plan B, 57
Planning, 36
Plateau mentality, 110
Power links. *See* www.womenwork-
    ing.com
Priorities, 45–46, 113
Procrastination, 90
Pros/cons of taking a risk, 37–41

Relationship, 114–115
Relin, Roz, 74
Research, 36, 71
Resiliency, 83
Richards, Ellen Swallow, 14, 106
Risk evaluation table, 101–102
Risk quotient, 36–48
    gut sense, 46–48
    priorities, 45–46
    pros/cons of taking a risk, 37–41
    timing, 42–46
Risk quotient balance sheet, 37–41,
    111

Risk-taker quiz, 49–50
Risk-taker type, 48–50
Risk-taking network, 59–78
    approaching your prospects,
        68–72
    mutually beneficial relationships,
        72–73
    selecting your mentors, 66–68
Risk-taking strategies, 51–56
    ask for help, 54–56. *See also*
        Risk–taking network
    failure, 53–54
    intuition, 51–52
    just do it!, 56
Risk-Taking Survey, 187–194
    finances and risk, 194
    gender and risk-taking attitude,
        191–192
    job satisfaction, 188–189
    personal life and risks, 193
    planning a change?, 189
    refusal to take risks, 190
    risk-taking attitude, 190
    risk-taking strategies, 192
Roché, Joyce, 179–181
Roddick, Anita, 23
Roebling, Emily Warren, 103
Romantic relationships, 114–115

Safety network, 104–105
Schectman, Sheila, 131–132
Schildkraut, Deniz, 104
Schwartz, Elizabeth Robinson,
    109
Second-guessing, 89
Shapiro, Judith, 183–185
Share your expertise, 105
Siebert, Muriel, 10
Simmons, Ruth J., 114

Six-step program
   personal life, 114–116
   step 1 (goal setting), 3–30
   step 2 (risk quotient), 31–58
   step 3 (risk-taking network),
      59–78
   step 4 (taking action), 79–96
   step 5 (claim victory), 97–106
   step 6 (continuous action),
      107–117
Sowell, Shaunna, 175–177
Srere, Linda, 159–161
Success stories. *See* Biographical
   sketches
Survey. *See* Risk-Taking Survey
Switzer, Kathrine, 15

Telling others what you've accom-
   plished, 102–104
Tennyson, JoAnn, 99–100
Tereshkova, Valentina, 46, 106
Thomas, Brenda, 55
Timing, 42–46, 77, 112
Toot your own horn, 102–104
Trailblazer mentality, 105–106
Trailblazers
   Agassiz, Elizabeth Cabot Cary, 42
   Alvarado, Linda G., 89
   Ball, Lucille, 19
   Bancroft, Ann, 63
   Boit, Elizabeth, 69
   Crump, Diane, 72
   Ederle, Gertrude, 116
   Jones, Rochelle, 95
   Lin, Maya, 82
   Mink, Patsy Takemoto, 100
   Ochoa, Ellen, 8

Trailblazers *(Cont.)*:
   Perkins, Frances, 65
   Richards, Ellen Swallow, 14
   Roddick, Anita, 23
   Roebling, Emily Warren, 103
   Schwartz, Elizabeth Robinson,
      109
   Siebert, Muriel, 10
   Simmons, Ruth J., 114
   Switzer, Kathrine, 15
   Tereshkova, Valentina, 46
   Walters, Barbara, 51
   Winfrey, Oprah, 74
   Woodhull, Victoria Claflin, 35
Traskell, Deb, 103
Turtle, 50

Vializ-Briggs, Miriam, 171–173

Wall Street Rising, 47
Walters, Barbara, 51
Winfrey, Oprah, 74, 105
Wolschlag, Gayle, 10
Women and risk-taking. *See* Risk-
   Taking Survey
Women's networks, 104–105
Woodhull, Victoria Claflin, 35
www.womenworking.com links
   books, 78
   corporate women's groups, 106
   inspirational stories, 30
   lifestyle, 117
   member network, 96
   success strategies, 58
   videos of author's TV programs,
      199
   women's associations, etc., 106

ABOUT THE AUTHOR

Helene Lerner hosts Emmy Award–winning television programs on public television that cover a wide range of topics affecting women today. A former columnist for *New Woman* magazine and for the *New York Post*'s "Wellness Watch," she also has authored several books, including *Embrace Change, Finding Balance, Stress Breakers, Our Power as Women: Wisdom and Strategies of Highly Successful Women, Time for Me: A Burst of Energy for Busy Women,* and *What Makes a Strong Woman?*

Helene is the founder of the popular Web site www.women working.com, which features success strategies for advancing, leading, and navigating work/life, as well as a lifestyle section, tips for honing professional skills, power-networking contacts, books and more.

Her company, Creative Expansions, Inc. (CEI), is designed to help women actualize their potential. She coaches individuals, groups, and Fortune 500 clients on techniques to increase their effectiveness. A member of Phi Beta Kappa, she holds a Master's degree in education and an MBA in management sciences.

AUTHOR PHOTOGRAPH © SHONNA VALESKA

Helene is available for keynotes and seminars on Smart Risk-Taking and other topics. Contact her via e-mail at: helene@ womenworking.com

For more information on purchasing videos of Helene's television programs, go to this link on her Web site: www.women working.com/lerner/helene_tv.php

60-minute women's forums/videocassettes

Make It Happen: Mentors, Dreams, Success

Women Going Global

Rocking the Barriers

Women Working 2000 and Beyond

30-minute documentaries

Mothers and Sons: Raising Compassionate Men

Best Friends: The Power of Sisterhood

Fathers and Daughters: Journeys of the Heart

Heartbeat to Heartbeat: Women and Heart Disease

Pure Magic: The Mother-Daughter Bond, winner of a 2004 Gracie Award from American Women in Radio and Television

Phenomenal Voyage: Women and Technology

Choices over a Lifetime

Proud to Be a Girl, winner of a 2004 New York Emmy Award

Grab Hold of the Reins: Women and Cancer, winner of a 2003 Gracie Award from American Women in Radio and Television

Blazes of Light: Women Living with HIV/AIDS, an Emmy nominee and winner of a 2000 Gracie Award from American Women in Radio and Television

Osteoporosis: Breaking the Fall

Osteoporosis: Your Bones, Your Life, winner of a 1997 National Media Owl Award from the Retirement Research Foundation

Finding the Strength Within: Living with Cancer

Out of the Darkness: Women and Depression, winner of a 1999 New York Emmy Award and Winner of a 1999 Gracie Award from American Women in Radio and Television

Alzheimer's Disease: Descent into Silence

Courageous Portraits: Living with Cancer